T H E
ANTI-CELLULITE
D I E T

THE
ANTI-CELLULITE
DIET

*The Low-Fat Way
to Lose Pounds, Inches
and Ugly Bulges in 28 Days*

CHERYL HARTSOUGH, R.D., L.D.
WITH SUSAN PRICE

G. P. Putnam's Sons
NEW YORK

To Michael McVay, chef, friend, partner and teacher, for his many hours of developing recipes, appreciating orchids and gardening and pushing me to reach out in life.

—C.H.

To Barbara Price Heller, "the pretty sister," my best friend, who has given me support and understanding.

—S.P.

Chart on page 111 adapted from *Diet Free* by Charles Kuntzleman (Arbor Press, Spring Arbor, MI, 1981). Used by permission of the author.

G. P. Putnam's Sons
Publishers Since 1838
200 Madison Avenue
New York, NY 10016

Library of Congress Cataloging-in-Publication Data

Hartsough, Cheryl, date.
    The anti-cellulite diet : the low-fat way to lose pounds, inches, and ugly bulges in 28 days / Cheryl Hartsough with Susan Price.
        p. cm.
    ISBN 0-399-13637-1
    1. Low-fat diet. 2. Reducing diets. 3. Health. I. Price, Susan, date. II. Title.
BM237.7.H38 1991   90-25809 CIP
613.2'5—dc20

Printed in the United States of America

1   2   3   4   5   6   7   8   9   10

ACKNOWLEDGMENTS FROM CHERYL HARTSOUGH

MY HEARTFELT THANKS to my grandmother, Anna Hansell: keep on going, genetics is still very important to me! To the guinea pigs of my early attempts at cooking: my father, the late Edward (Ted) Hartsough, Jr. (not from my cooking); my mother, Anne; sisters Cathy Kollmer and Carol Wagner; brothers Ed, Steve and Bob Hartsough; and to the best cook, the late Regina (Jean) Hartsough. Also to the captain of my heart, Malcolm MacNeill, Jr., and his family.

To the many creative and inspiring professionals, friends and workout partners, especially Judy Perkins, Ph.D., R.D., who found time in her very busy schedule to proofread my work and help me through life professionally and personally; to the eternal optimist, my mentor Barbara Y. Tidwell, R.D.; to Joseph Barone, M.S., a very special friend; to the kindhearted Gwen Ritter, M.P.H., who has helped many people strive for wellness; also to Sue Olney Beck, R.N.; Kara Burke, R.N.; Roxanne Salas; Kathy Casper; Laurie Mikus; Sue DeMarco Long; Vicki Masucci West; Steve Capellini; Bill Scrogins; Jack Rudin and Phyllis Schnurmacher. There are countless others who have been supportive of me since my youth, from my Girl Scout leader, Mrs. Jackie Bolger, to the late Dorothy (Dot) Baxter, who always believed in me, even when I didn't. And to my second families: the Burkes, Thompsons, and Mullens of Roslyn, Pennsylvania. THANK YOU.

Acknowledgments from Cheryl Hartsough

A special thanks from both of us to Andrea Chambers at Putnam, who made this book possible, and to her able assistant Dolores McMullan.

And finally, our literary agent and friend Stuart Krichevsky, a young gentleman of the old school, and his helpful right hand, Bill Spruill.

ACKNOWLEDGMENTS FROM SUSAN PRICE

I WOULD LIKE to thank my mother, Sabina L. Price, for setting me on the right track with early admonishments to "eat an apple instead of a Twinkie, drink a glass of water instead of a soda and take a walk instead of sitting in front of the TV." And thank you to Camille Cozzone and Nancy Dinsmore for their professional encouragement and personal friendship, to John Edwards for getting me "on line" fast, and the people at Outbound Computer who were there when I needed them most. Also to my dermatologist, Dr. Letantia Bussell, who helped me separate advertising hyperbole from scientific truth about cellulite remedies, Kerstin Florian for sharing her vast experience, Todd and Robin Del Pesco of L.A. Private Trainers, Julie Anthony of the Aspen Club, and Shari Williams, Heidi Koper and Cari Bjeljac of the Santa Monica Athletic Club, who have motivated me to keep working out and have fun doing it.

I am grateful also to Peter Vash, president of the American Bariatrics Association, for all his generous time, wisdom and knowledge; to Johanna Dwyer, D.Sc., R.D., director of the Frances Stern Center at New England Medical Center and Dr. Maria Simonson, director of the Health, Weight and Stress Clinic at Johns Hopkins Medical Institution, for their heartfelt cooperation and for sharing their research and information.

CONTENTS

CONTENTS

ONE

AN INTRODUCTION
The Bottom Line on Cellulite

WHO AMONG US hasn't found herself standing in a department-store dressing room, dreading to look at the rear view in the mirror? As we scrutinize our bodies in that fluorescent glare that seems to magnify every bump and ripple, what most of us loathe is that dimpled, puckered flesh on the hips and thighs. You've probably heard this condition disparaged as "pincushion" or "cottage-cheese" thighs. The correct term is cellulite, pronounced cell-u-*leet* because of the French origins of the word. Whatever you may call it, you'd rather not have it. Fortunately, cellulite can be reduced sanely, safely and without starvation, spot reducing—or surgery.

This book is all about cellulite: the facts, the fiction and the battle plan. The diet we offer is not just a quick fix, but an intelligent strategy to burn fat and increase your metabolism. Incorporating the most scientific, up-to-date information, the Anti-Cellulite Diet is designed to get you on a sound eating plan not just for now, but for life. After 28 days on the program, you will see a major improvement in your body and feel a lot more comfortable about the way you look in a bathing suit. You will also feel stronger, healthier and more energetic. And, if you successfully alter your eating habits and start exercising (see Chapter 6), you may even live longer and will certainly live better.

Let's begin by dispelling some myths.

There is nothing exotic or mysterious about cellulite. It is simply fat like any other. However, cellulite is more likely to accumulate on fleshy areas of the body, such as the hips and buttocks. In these problem spots, the fibrous connecting bands that attach to the skin and muscles form a sort of netting that covers the fat cells. As these fat cells enlarge, they push through the spaces in the "netting" and cause the bulges that show up as dimpled flesh.

Cellulite has been around forever, kept discreetly out of sight by fashion and mores. However, the term itself is relatively new. It was coined in the 1970s, when all those bikini-clad women appeared on the beaches of Saint-Tropez. The French dubbed this newly exposed fat "cellulite"; the word eventually found its way into *Webster's,* where it is defined as "lumpy fat found in the thighs, hips, and buttocks of some women."

WHY DO WOMEN GET CELLULITE?

Blame it on biology. Those fat stores found mostly on hips and buttocks are nature's way of building up lactational fat. Women need some fat stores to produce hormones for pregnancy and breast-feeding. Men are generally spared cellulite because they are not genetically programmed to produce and conserve this kind of fat. Moreover, their fibrous tissue is denser. Women, however, *need* a certain amount of body fat to maintain smooth, supple skin, glossy hair and natural feminine curves. They also require body fat to menstruate. Women whose composition of body fat falls below 11 percent may stop getting their periods; they may also suffer from the premature bone loss known as osteoporosis.

Obviously, women must strike a balance between having too much fat and not enough on their bodies. This book will teach you how to reduce *excess body fat* and hence, cellulite.

Your fat cells themselves are like your shadow; they are with you for life. Only the seriously obese have not only *larger* cells, but *more* of them. For most women, the difference in appearance between slim and overweight comes from the increased size of the cells themselves as they soak up the fat that floats through the bloodstream.

THE FAT-GRAM FACTOR

Merely lowering your caloric intake will not necessarily shrink fat cells. What *does* help is limiting the number of fat grams you eat to less than 20 percent of your calories. This formula, in conjunction with a program of low-intensity aerobic exercise, works!

On the Anti-Cellulite Diet, you eat approximately 15 grams of fat a day. This is carefully calculated to keep you feeling healthy and fit. This is *not* a starvation diet. You will be eating between 1,000 and 1,300 calories a day, an amount that will keep your metabolic rate from dropping, as it often does temporarily on very low-calorie diets. If your metabolism stays up, it's easier to lose weight.

LOSE FAT, NOT WATER

On the diet, you will lose 1 to 2 pounds of fat per week—that's *fat,* not water. (Women who need to lose *more* weight are likely to show a greater drop on the scale the first week than women with less weight to lose. That's because of differences in water loss.)

Not only will you lose weight on this diet and exercise regime, you won't feel deprived. As we've learned, one reason women overeat is because of a sense of emotional deprivation. Traditional diets only *compound* that sense of loss. The Anti-Cellulite Diet does not ask you to give up everything you have loved to eat and subsist on rabbit food or liquid meals. That kind of dieting only sets you up for a major slip and can lead to the self-destructive bingeing that put on the pounds in the first place.

YOU'RE ONLY HUMAN

There are times when you just *have* to have that cookie, glass of wine or dab of peanut butter. The Anti-Cellulite Diet actually *allows* for that kind of perfectly acceptable indulgence—*as long as it is within reason.* You will find built-in "pressure valves" for those times when you feel ready to "blow it." So, on certain days, you can go ahead and eat a few candies or cookies. As long as these treats are calibrated into the total fat allowance, it's okay.

Remember, what matters is not so much *calories* as *fat.* Even if you eat ten peanut *M&M's* or sip a glass of wine once a week, you can still lose weight, smooth out your cellulite and feel better and stronger each day. Because you are not deprived, you will find it easier to stop that yo-yo cycle of losing weight, bingeing and gaining it all back.

"FORBIDDEN FOODS" CAN BE OKAY

Eating is actually *fun* on the Anti-Cellulite Diet and subsequent maintenance plan (Chapter 4). Instead of those routine, boring diet meals (plain broiled fish, dry toast, endless lettuce salads), you dine on satisfying gourmet dishes that are easy to prepare (see the forty-five recipes in Chapter 8). The emphasis of the diet is on basic fresh foods, including those once thought of as "forbidden," such as baked potatoes, salmon mousse, raisins, even lasagna. You'll find menus that minimize the amount of time spent in food preparation and maximize the availability of tasty nutritious meals. For example, you might create a delicious main dinner one night and then make some "spin-offs" for subsequent meals. You could perhaps bake a barbecued-chicken dish on Monday and mix the leftover chicken with some other ingredients in a pita pocket a day or two later.

You will also learn to save time and effort by preparing big batches of foods such as low-fat lasagna (p. 148) and then freezing portion-size packets that can be reheated in minutes in an oven or microwave. Hence, you reduce the temptations of repeated exposure to food at dinnertime, when you're vulnerable.

THE ANTI-CELLULITE BAR

For those times when you're on the run and even a minute is more than you can spare, you can munch on an Anti-Cellulite Bar, a high-fiber, nutrition-packed pick-me-up that you can make in batches, wrap individually and store in an airtight container. Just toss one in your purse or keep some in your glove compartment or desk drawer for those moments when you need a quick fix without blowing your diet.

WHY IT WORKS

The biggest breakthrough in weight control in recent years is the discovery that fat grams count more than calories. This remarkable finding came about as a by-product of an eating plan devised at Harvard for breast-cancer patients. Because a low-fat diet can reduce the estrogen that many tumors need to grow, doctors told patients to cut fat—though not necessarily calories—from their diet. Weight loss came as a surprise bonus.

In another research project at Harvard in 1987, doctors conducted a study of 5,000 women who had been athletes in college. They found that these women had a substantially lower lifetime risk of breast and other cancers than did the general population. The reason, they surmised, was that the athletes tended to have a leaner body mass than did women in the control group; they also ate less fat. The low-fat diet, doctors concluded, helped keep estrogen levels from rising and hence reduced the risk of certain cancers. Though the exact correlation between fat ingestion and cancer is still in the research stages, there is a strong indication that a fatty diet is not a healthy diet.

REASONS TO LOSE FAT TODAY

Losing fat is clearly important not only for beauty but for health. At least one quarter of all Americans have more than 20 percent extra fat on their bodies. This increases their chances of suffering various diseases, including heart ailments, diabetes and some kinds of cancer.

- Fat loves company. The greater the amount of fat you allow to accumulate on your body, the more likely you are to get more. When fat replaces muscle, you burn fewer calories and have less strength and energy to stay active.
- Fat makes it harder to get all the vital nutrients we need and still maintain an ideal weight because a fat

16

body is a body with a sluggish metabolism. The lower the metabolism, the fewer vitamins and minerals you get because you have to eat very little to avoid gaining weight.

Fat lowers our self-esteem. Probably the worst thing about gaining fat is what it does to our self-image. Sure, surgery is an option, but wouldn't you rather know you've got the power to control and shape your own body?

HOW COME TWO WOMEN WHO WEIGH THE SAME CAN LOOK SO DIFFERENT?

One woman may have a body as smooth and sleek as a cat's; another may look puffy and pudgy, with thighs rippled with cellulite, yet both weigh the same. The reason? The woman with the catlike shape has a lower percentage of fat and a higher percentage of lean muscle mass in her body. Fat takes up five times the space of muscle, but muscle weighs more than fat. A pound of muscle burns up to three times more calories an hour than a pound of fat!

HOW TO DETERMINE YOUR LEAN/FAT RATIO

Sports doctors and trained exercise physiologists administer various sophisticated tests to determine a person's lean/fat ratio. At gyms and spas, trained staffers work with a piece of equipment called a caliper. The qualified staff member gently pinches your folds of fat with the caliper and tells you the results.

You can try the basic "pinch test" at home to learn how much excess fat you have on your body. Holding your fingers vertically, pinch:

- the front of your thigh
- the back of your upper arm
- your waistline
- your stomach
- under your shoulder blades

If you can pinch more than an inch in any of these places, you may have excess body fat.

The chart below indicates the optimal percentages of body fat for women:

Lean	Good	Average	Needs Improvement	Poor
18%	19–22%	23–26%	27–29%	>30%

SUMMING UP

To many women, cellulite is unattractive and stubborn. Spot reducing exercises do not work to reduce cellulite. Nor does simply lowering your caloric intake necessarily improve matters. What *does* help, however, is a combination of fat-burning aerobic exercise in a low-intensity range and the lowering of fat grams in your diet. Together these can help "shrink" fat cells in your body, resulting in a slimmer, sleeker you.

In the next chapter, you will be introduced to the principles of the Anti-Cellulite Diet and learn why and how the program works!

TWO

GETTING READY
The Diet Principles and How They Work

THE ANTI-CELLULITE DIET is based on the very simple concept of maintaining a regular exercise program (see Chapter 6) and eating the right low-fat foods at frequent intervals throughout the day. You've learned by now that fat is not your friend. Eating a pint of fat-laden ice cream or a bag of chocolate-chip cookies is going to increase your cellulite. In some measure, this is because fat is very easy for the body to absorb. It sails through your digestive system with ease; 95 percent of the fat you consume is absorbed by the body, whereas carbohydrates and protein use up approximately 20 percent of their own calories merely to be digested, leaving only 80 percent of their calories behind.

This means that you are better off eating protein and carbohydrates than fat. Think of carbohydrates and lean protein as *foods that eat themselves.* Carbohydrates are also important because they help build up stores of glycogen in the liver and muscles, which enhances energy and stamina. This is why the Anti-Cellulite Diet is high in carbohydrates, particularly complex ones like cereals and grains that take longer to digest. Moreover, the diet emphasizes carbohydrates at dinner. Research (including studies done at the Massachusetts Institute of Technology) has shown that the production of carbohydrates increases tryptophan, an amino acid that has a calming effect and helps some people sleep more soundly.

YOU'LL EAT SIX MEALS A DAY

On this diet plan, you'll be eating breakfast, lunch and dinner, plus three special snacks a day. The midmorning treat provides a needed boost to keep blood sugar up until lunch. The afternoon snack augments the effects of the protein and carbohydrates you had at lunch to prevent that "out-of-gas" feeling most people experience between 3 and 5 P.M. And an evening snack keeps you from making nocturnal raids on the refrigerator. Small, frequent meals full of complex carbohydrates keep the body from storing fat as readily. Don't skip any of these opportunities to eat because each one is an important part of the diet and nutrition strategy.

Many of the snack suggestions in this program are high in calcium. Women *need* calcium and it is absorbed better when it is not competing with other nutrients in the metabolic process. You'll find lots of non-fat yogurt, "Smoothies" (non-fat versions of strawberry milk shakes) and skim milk on this diet.

There are no "empty-calorie" sugar snacks on this diet because they can trigger a sugar craving (some research shows that even artificial sweeteners do this). More important, the "high" some people feel after eating sugar gives way to a "low" one hour later as the blood-sugar level drops. This sense of hunger and irritability is a danger point for dieters. All the hard-won gains can disappear with one big food binge.

YOU CAN EVEN "BLOW IT"—SAFELY—WITH BUILT-IN "PRESSURE VALVES"

Of course, everybody "blows" their diet at some point. So instead of ignoring this reality and leaving you on your own to feel guilty when you binge (and possibly binge even more from the anxiety caused by "blowing it"), we've built in "pressure valves." With these you can "blow it" without blowing it, and let off steam when you need to. Once a week, on Day Six, you will have one "pressure valve" that is the equivalent of 100 calories and 5 grams of fat. This could be a 4-ounce glass of wine, two cookies, three caramels, ten peanut *M&M's,* one-third of a (1.65-ounce) Hershey's bar, two-thirds of a Weight Watchers ice-cream sandwich or your own personal favorite "comfort" food—as long as it contains no more than 100 calories and 5 grams of fat.

THE BASICS OF THE ANTI-CELLULITE DIET PLAN

BE PRUDENT

Before starting a diet or exercise program, you should always consult with your physician.

LIMIT CAFFEINE TO TWO SERVINGS PER DAY OF THE FOLLOWING

- iced tea
- coffee
- tea

DRINK

At least eight glasses of water each day. If you don't like plain water, buy non-sodium seltzer or sparkling water. And limit caffeine-free herbal teas to two a day. (While some herbal teas are diuretics, we still don't know all their other effects on the body.)

Plain water is actually a wonderful aid to weight loss. It aids the kidneys in flushing impurities out of the system, reducing the dehydration that causes skin to appear dry and lined. At Johns Hopkins Medical Center, researchers have found that drinking a glass of water ten minutes before eating triggers a feeling of fullness faster and after fewer calories.

THINK OF ALCOHOL AS "FAT IN A BOTTLE"

Though alcohol does not actually contain fat grams, it is almost as dense in calories as fat and metabolizes very much the same way. It is not a quick pick-me-up, as some people think, because the body does not use it as readily as it absorbs carbohydrates. Another reason that the diet does not contain alcohol is because it affects your judgment about food selection and lowers inhibitions about how much you eat. Even moderate alcohol intake is the enemy of weight control. Alcohol contains no nutrients and adds 62,116 calories a year to the diet of the average American social drinker—nearly eighteen pounds!

SUPPLEMENT THE DIET WITH

- one 100-percent-RDA multivitamin-and-mineral tablet in the losing phase of the diet to ensure that you're getting all the amounts of vitamins and minerals recommended daily.
- one 500-mg. calcium supplement

LAY IN A STORE OF ANTI-CELLULITE BARS

These delicious bars, made with dried fruits and wholesome grains, are your protection against bingeing. Keep them handy at home, in your purse, in your car or in your desk drawer for those times when you're hungry and need a quick pick-me-up. Unlike most of the so-called "diet" and "energy" bars on the market today, the Anti-

Cellulite Bar is low in calories and very low in fat. It is loaded with complex carbohydrates, the best source for quick available energy. It will keep you feeling good and help you avoid the hunger pangs, headaches and fatigue that occur with most diets. By having one at snacktime, you will approach mealtimes with your appetite under control—thus preventing the common diet trap of getting so hungry all day that you lose control and blow it at dinner.

EAT

Breakfast

- One serving of fruit: choice of ½ grapefruit, ¼ cantaloupe, ¾ cup strawberries or 1 orange
- One to two servings of bread or cereal: one serving = 1 regular or 2 thin slices of bread (whole-wheat or multigrain is best); ¾ cup whole grain cereal flakes; ½ English muffin; ½ bagel
- ½ cup skim milk
- Coffee or tea (herbal or regular)

Morning snack

- Fruit or Anti-Cellulite Bar

Lunch

- One 2–3-oz. serving of protein: choice of lean meats or fish
- One cup of salad: includes dark-green lettuce, 2 slices of tomato, nonfat salad dressing
- One ½-cup serving of cooked vegetables: broccoli, green beans or carrots, or one cup of raw vegetables
- One serving whole-grain bread or equivalent
- One serving of fruit

Midafternoon snack

- One-half serving of dairy: ½ cup of nonfat yogurt, or
- 5 cups air-popped popcorn, or
- One cup of raw vegetables with mustard dip, or
- One-half serving of fruit: ½ orange, 1 small peach, 1 dried fig, 1 oz. raisins

Dinner

- One 2–3-oz. serving of protein: lean meat, fish or poultry
- One cup of cooked vegetables or two cups raw vegetables
- One to two servings of starch: 1 medium potato, ⅔ cup of corn, 1 cup pasta, or ½ cup rice
- One-half serving of fruit

Evening snack

- ¾ cup nonfat frozen yogurt, or ½ cup special Anti-Cellulite Smoothie or 1 cup skim milk, or
- any midafternoon snack

Naturally, some days you will have slightly more protein at one meal than another, or you might vary the formula slightly. However, these are basic guidelines: try to keep track of what you eat and start knowing what foods are in each group. Pay close attention to the fat-gram counter in Chapter 9. Eventually, you will reeducate yourself. Remember all those years you wouldn't eat pasta because you thought it was fattening? By studying the fat-gram counter, you'll learn that pasta itself is just fine—as long as you have it with a low-fat tomato sauce, not a creamy one!

A QUICK DIET OVERVIEW

The following chart is a very general guide to approximate servings of the basic foods allowed on the diet: The 1,000 to 1,300 calorie count approximates that of the diet.

Calories	Protein (ounces)	Dairy (servings)	Fruit (servings)	Veg (servings)	Starch (servings)	Fat (servings)
1000	4	2	2	3	4	.5 tsp.
1200	4	3	2	3	4	1 tsp.
1300	5	3	3	4	4	1 tsp.

DON'T BE A SLAVE TO YOUR DIET

Everybody's different and no matter how perfect a diet may be in theory, no diet is perfect if *you* can't stay on it. A diet you can live with on an ongoing basis has to be customized to your own needs, habits and preferences. Consult the suggested substitutions in Chapter 9. Use them to devise a lifetime eating plan that works for you!

THREE

THE ANTI-CELLULITE DIET
Four Weeks to a Better Body

THE BASICS

1. Drink eight 8-ounce glasses of water each day (tap water with a squeeze of fresh lemon or low-sodium sparkling water or seltzer). In addition, you can have two of the following beverages a day: iced tea, herbal tea, hot coffee. Limit diet sodas to one a day, but try to do without.

2. No alcohol except on bonus day, when four ounces of wine are allowed.

3. Note that we often give you choices on the diet plan. (For example, we might suggest a recipe from Chapter 8 as well as a more basic alternative that does not require a recipe.) Remember: *these are choices. You can have one or the other, not both!*

4. Now and then, you may be too tired to cook or you may want to try an acceptable deviation from the diet plan. You can always have a 300–350-calorie low-fat frozen dinner such as Lean Cuisine, Pritikin, Weight Watchers or Healthy Choice. Don't exceed 10 grams of fat or 800 mg. of sodium. Or, for lunch, fix yourself a fruit plate with one cup of cottage cheese (try for a 1-percent-fat brand) or have a cup of tossed salad greens with low-fat dressing and 3 to 5 ounces of broiled fish or chicken. For

dinner, try a cup of pasta with 4 ounces of red sauce, a cup of steamed vegetables and a cup of salad greens with low-fat dressing. If you feel like dessert, fresh fruit, a half cup of nonfat frozen yogurt or two graham crackers are good choices.

5. If you have plans to dine out at lunch or dinner, you can still follow the diet. Just order the fruit plate mentioned above. Or ask for plain broiled fish or chicken (3 to 5 ounces is a portion roughly equivalent to the diameter of your palm and the thickness of the knuckle on your pinkie), and a big salad with oil and vinegar on the side. Also, refer to the dining-out tips in Chapter 4.

6. Keep plenty of the Anti-Cellulite Bars on hand. (Store them in an airtight container, individually wrapped.) Enjoy them as is or warm them up in a toaster oven. Or keep a low-fat commercial bran muffin on hand (about 2½″ by 2½″) if you don't feel like cooking.

7. Take a 100%-RDA vitamin supplement daily as well as a 500-mg. calcium supplement.

WEEK ONE

Day 1

	Calories	Fat Grams
Breakfast:		
1 Anti-Cellulite Bar (p. 128) **or** small, low-fat bran muffin **or** 1½ slices of whole-grain bread with 1 tsp. apple butter (p. 160)	145	1
¼ cantaloupe	50	0
Snack:		
½ cup skim milk	45	0
Lunch:		
1 cup lemon chicken consommé (skim fat from low-sodium broth or buy Pritikin or another nonfat brand; add slice of lemon)	20	0
5 oz. snapper (or any white fish)	180	2
broiled with 1 tsp. butter **or** margarine	35	4
6 spears asparagus	20	0
¾ cup strawberries **or** ½ cup cantaloupe	30	0

	Calories	Fat Grams
Snack:		
½ cup nonfat plain yogurt	55	0
½ fruit (small banana **or** medium apple)	40	0
Dinner:		
1 cup cooked spaghetti with 4 oz. Ragú Homestyle Sauce & 2 cups added diced vegetables **or** 1 cup pasta with Red Sauce (p. 148)	320	5
½ zucchini marinated with 2 Tbsp. balsamic vinegar, ½ tsp. capers, 1 thin slice onion and topped with chopped fresh parsley **or** tossed green salad w/ 1 Tbsp. nonfat dressing	20	1
1 cup diced mango **or** 3 oz. nonfat frozen yogurt	105	0
Snack:		
1 dried fig **or** 2 Tbsp. raisins	50	0
TOTAL:	1115 (10.5% fat)	13

NOTE: Recipes appear in Chapter 8.

DAY TWO

	Calories	Fat Grams
Breakfast:		
1 oz. Shredded Wheat (or whole-wheat low-sugar cereal)	90	0
½ cup skim milk	45	0
½ small banana	40	0
Snack:		
½ cup grapefruit juice	40	0
Lunch:		
Anti-Cellulite Tuna Salad (Combine 3 oz. drained tuna in water with ½ Tbsp. Weight Watchers mayonnaise, ½ cup low-fat cottage cheese, 1 chopped stalk celery, 1 Tbsp. chopped scallions, 1 Tbsp. lemon juice, ½ Tbsp. chopped parsley and a pinch of pepper. Serve in a medium tomato with ½ orange slice for garnish.)	245	3

	Calories	Fat Grams
Snack:		
1 Anti-Cellulite Bar (p. 128) **or** 10 flavored mini rice cakes	145	1
Dinner:		
3 oz. chicken breast marinated in ½ Tbsp. honey and 1 Tbsp. chopped fresh basil or 1 tsp. dried basil, ½ Tbsp. light soy sauce, 1 Tbsp. Dijon mustard, ¼ cup raspberry vinegar, a pinch of thyme and black pepper	170	4
½ cup cooked brown rice (cook ¼ cup brown rice in ½ cup chicken broth or water)	110	0
1 cup salad greens with 1 Tbsp. nonfat dressing	20	0
½ cup cooked string beans mixed with 2 slices chopped fresh tomatoes sauteed in Pam with ½ clove garlic, black pepper to taste	45	0
Snack:		
½ cup nonfat yogurt with 1 tsp. all-fruit, no-sugar jam	70	0
TOTAL:	1020	8
		(7% fat)

DAY THREE

	Calories	Fat Grams
Breakfast:		
1 Lender's raisin bagel (**or** ⅔ Sara Lee)	165	1
1-oz. wedge low-fat cheese	45	3
½ grapefruit	40	0
Snack:		
½ fruit (lg. orange **or** med. apple)	40	0
Lunch:		
2 oz. chicken (cook extra at dinner on Day Two) in med. pita with lettuce & 2 slices tomato	250	4
1 Tbsp. honey mustard or Dijon	10	1
½ cup sliced cucumber in low-cal vinaigrette **or** 2 cups raw broccoli	40	0
½ fruit (orange **or** apple)	40	0
Snack:		
1 oz. (2 Tbsp.) raisins	50	0

	Calories	Fat Grams
Dinner:		
3 oz. grilled lean sirloin steak with ½ medium potato with mustard & 1 cup steamed mushrooms	280	9
1 roasted red pepper with ½ tsp. capers and 1 tsp. balsamic vinegar	20	0
1 medium peach (**or** 2 prunes **or** 1 sm. plum)	40	0
Snack:		
½ cup skim milk **or** nonfat yogurt **or** Anti-Cellulite Smoothie (1 cup frozen strawberries w/o syrup, ½ ripe banana, ½ cup skim milk, ½ cup plain nonfat yogurt, add few ice cubes, blend all till smooth. Serves four ½-cup servings; eat one portion, freeze rest.)	50	0
TOTAL:	1070	18
		(15% fat)

DAY FOUR

	Calories	Fat Grams
Breakfast:		
¼ cantaloupe	50	0
1 regular slice whole-wheat bread (**or** 2 thin)	70	1
2 tsp. peanut butter	65	6
1 tsp. honey	20	0
Snack:		
1 lg. rice cake with 1 Tbsp. apple butter	75	0
Lunch:		
Big Salad (2 cups greens, cup spinach, mushrooms, shredded carrots, cup broccoli, tomato, ½ cup garbanzo beans, ½ cup water chestnuts, 2 oz. chicken breast, 2 Tbsp. no-oil dressing)	380	6

	Calories	Fat Grams
Snack:		
1 med. peach **or** ½ cup blueberries **or** ¾ cup raspberries	40	0
Dinner:		
1 cup spaghetti with 4 oz. White-Clam and Shrimp Sauce (p. 145) **or** 1 cup pasta with 4 oz. Ragú sauce mixed with 3 oz. chicken, turkey or any fish or shellfish	365	7
Tomato and basil salad w/ balsamic vinegar	50	0
1 cup broccoli, steamed or microwaved	40	0
Snack:		
½ cup Anti-Cellulite Smoothie (diet p. 33)	50	0
TOTAL:	1205	20
		(15% fat)

DAY FIVE

	Calories	Fat Grams
Breakfast:		
¾ cup *Nutri-Grain* whole-wheat cereal **or** ¾ cup Shredded Wheat	100	0
2 Tbsp. raisins	50	0
½ cup skim milk	45	0
2 Tbsp. nonfat plain yogurt, served on cereal	15	0
Snack:		
½ fruit (lg. orange, apple **or** 12 grapes)	40	0
Lunch:		
3 oz. (roughly 15 med.) peeled shrimp, broiled or boiled, served chilled w/ lemon, **or** 2 oz. turkey breast	105	1
2 cups raw vegetables (carrots, broccoli, cauliflower, green and red pepper)	80	0
2 oz. Veg Dip (1 Tbsp. Dijon mustard, mixed w/ 3 Tbsp. nonfat yogurt and ½ Tbsp. chopped scallions	20	0

	Calories	Fat Grams
Snack:		
1 med. apple	80	0
Dinner:		
Pita Pizza (use 2 oz. leftover Red Sauce (p. 148) on both open-face halves of a whole-wheat pita; add ½ oz. part-skim mozzarella to each half and ½ cup mushrooms, green and red peppers on top)	250	6
½ cup blueberries **or** blackberries, **or** ¾ cup raspberries **or** 1 cup strawberries	40	0
Snack:		
½ cup nonfat plain yogurt, mixed with	55	0
½ small sliced banana	40	0
TOTAL:	920	7
		(7% fat)

DAY SIX

It's time for a treat! You get a bonus of 100 calories and 5 grams of fat: a 4-oz. glass of wine, 2 small cookies, 3 caramels, 10 peanut *M&M's,* ⅓ of a Hershey's chocolate bar (1.65-oz. only) **or** ⅔ Weight Watchers ice-cream sandwich. Eat it whenever you want and *bon appétit!*

	Calories	Fat Grams
Breakfast:		
1 Anti-Cellulite Bar (p. 128) **or** ¾ English muffin **or** 1½ slices whole-grain bread w/ 1 Tbsp. apple butter or all-fruit jam	145	1
½ grapefruit	40	0
Snack:		
½ cup grapefruit juice **or** ½ grapefruit	40	0
Lunch:		
½ cantaloupe	95	0
1 cup 1% low-fat cottage cheese	160	3
½ cup strawberries	20	0

	Calories	Fat Grams
Snack:		
5 flavored mini rice cakes **or** 2 large rice cakes	70	0
1 oz. wedge of low-fat cheese	45	3
Dinner:		
3 ½ oz. skinless turkey breast, roasted	155	3
1 baked sweet potato w/ 1 Tbsp. honey mustard	125	0
½ cup (5 spears) asparagus	15	0
½ cup unsweetened applesauce w/ cinnamon	55	0
Snack:		
½ serving Simplesse "fake fat" ice cream.	60	0
TOTAL:	1025	10
		(9% fat)
With special snack:	1125	15
		(12% fat)

DAY SEVEN

	Calories	Fat Grams

Breakfast:

	Calories	Fat Grams
3 Egg-White Omelet (Spray non-stick pan with Pam; whip egg whites and cook for 30 seconds; add ½ cup steamed spinach, onion, pepper or a combination, onto one half of the egg, flip empty half over to cover vegetables; cook 2 minutes)	70	0
1 slice whole-wheat bread with	70	1
1 tsp. all-fruit, no-sugar jam	15	0
2 prunes **or** ½ grapefruit	40	0

Snack:

	Calories	Fat Grams
1-oz. wedge of cheese with Akmak cracker	65	3

Lunch:

	Calories	Fat Grams
2 oz. leftover turkey breast on pita with ¼ cup sprouts, 3 asparagus spears, ¼ cup shredded carrots	255	3
1 Tbsp. low-fat bottled ranch dressing	35	3
½ apple	40	0

	Calories	Fat Grams
Snack:		
1 Anti-Cellulite Bar (p. 128) **or** 6 cups air-popped popcorn	145	1
Dinner:		
Potato, Tomato and String Bean Special		
Large twice-baked gourmet potato (mix pre-baked potato pulp with 2 Tbsp. 1% cottage cheese, a pinch of cayenne pepper, 1 Tbsp scallions, 1 Tbsp. grated Parmesan, 1 tsp. minced onion, pinch of garlic powder, 2 Tbsp. Dijon mustard; season with a pinch of black pepper and marjoram; restuff and top with paprika; bake again for 20 min. at 350 degrees.)	205	5
1 tomato, sliced in half and topped with 2 tsp. bread crumbs, 1 tsp. Parmesan, and ½ tsp. parsley, and broiled for 10 minutes	75	1
1 cup string beans	40	0
Snack:		
1 oz. Anti-Cellulite Smoothie (diet p. 33)	50	0
TOTAL:	1105	17
		(14% fat)

41

WEEK TWO

DAY ONE

	Calories	Fat Grams
Breakfast:		
1 cup nonfat plain yogurt	110	0
½ cup fresh **or** frozen blueberries	40	0
1 Tbsp. *Grape-Nuts* **or** any crunchy cereal	20	0
Snack:		
1 Anti-Cellulite Bar (p. 128) **or** 2 graham crackers and a ½ small banana	145	1
Lunch:		
Turkey Pasta (2 oz. turkey, ¾ cup cooked mini-shell pasta with 1 cup raw vegetables tossed with 1 tsp. olive oil, 2 Tbsp. balsamic vinegar and Italian herbs)	285	7
1 orange	60	0

	Calories	Fat Grams
Snack:		
1 rice cake with 1 Tbsp. jam **or** apple butter	75	0
Dinner:		
5 oz. Salmon w/ Yogurt Dill Sauce (p. 140) **or** 5 oz. broiled white fish with 1 tsp. butter or margarine	260	12
½ cup cooked carrots mixed with 1 tsp. honey and mint	40	0
½ cup sliced cucumber and onion in low-cal vinaigrette	20	0
Snack:		
12 fresh **or** frozen grapes	40	0
TOTAL:	1095 (16.5% fat)	20

DAY TWO

	Calories	Fat Grams
Breakfast:		
1 Anti-Cellulite Bar (p. 128) **or** English muffin with 1 Tbsp. all-fruit jam	145	1
¼ cantaloupe	50	0
Snack:		
3 dried apricots	45	0
Lunch:		
4 oz. canned crab served on 2 cups spinach, mixed with 1 chopped, cooked egg white, 1 cup sliced mushrooms, and 2 Tbsp. nonfat ranch dressing	160	4
1 small sliced apple	60	0
6 Melba rounds, 6 Kavli crackers **or** 4 Akmak crackers	90	1

	Calories	Fat Grams
Snack:		
1 fruit kabob (4 chunks pineapple, 3 cherries) **or** ¾ cup cantaloupe	45	0
Dinner:		
4 oz. Baked Snapper with Mustard (p. 141) **or** snapper (or other white fish) baked with 1 oz. white wine	140	2
1 cup beef or chicken broth with chopped cilantro, dill **or** chives	20	0
Tossed salad greens with no-oil dressing	20	0
1 cup steamed summer squash, with parsley	25	0
½ cup cooked brown rice (¼ cup raw brown in ½ cup chicken broth or water)	110	0
Snack:		
½ cup skim milk **or** nonfat yogurt or Smoothie (diet p. 33) (add 5 calories for Smoothie)	45	0
TOTAL:	955 (7.5% fat)	8

DAY THREE

	Calories	Fat Grams
Breakfast:		
¾ cup whole-wheat flake cereal **or** 1 cup Shredded Wheat	100	0
½ banana	40	0
½ cup skim milk	45	0
1 Tbsp. raisins	25	0
Snack:		
½ cup unsweetened applesauce with a sprinkle of cinnamon	55	0
Lunch:		
Peanut Butter & Jelly Sandwich (2 slices whole-wheat bread, 1 Tbsp. peanut butter, 1 tsp. no-sugar, all-fruit jam)	270	10
1 orange	60	0

	Calories	Fat Grams
Snack:		
½ cup skim milk **or** yogurt	45	0
Dinner:		
3 oz. chicken baked with 1 Tbsp. Dijon mustard or Barbecued Chicken (p. 138)	170	4
Tossed green salad with no-oil dressing	20	0
Carrot Salad (½ cup shredded carrots and 1 tsp. raisins, mixed with 1 tsp. light mayonnaise & 1 tsp. nonfat yogurt)	75	2
Corn on the cob with 1 tsp. butter **or** margarine	105	5
Snack:		
1 oz. (2 Tbsp.) raisins	50	0
TOTAL:	1060	21
	(18% fat)	

DAY FOUR

	Calories	Fat Grams
Breakfast:		
1 cup oatmeal with cinnamon & 1 tsp. raisins	165	2
½ cup skim milk	45	0
½ cup unsweetened applesauce	50	0
Snack:		
2 prunes	40	0
Lunch:		
Leftover 3 oz. chicken on greens with ½ cup canned artichoke hearts	235	4
Crudités of ½ cup raw vegetables served with dip of 2 Tbsp. mustard, 2 Tbsp. yogurt and 2 Tbsp. chives	65	1
1 small whole-grain roll or 4 Akmak crackers	80	1

THE ANTI-CELLULITE DIET

	Calories	Fat Grams
Snack:		
½ cup nonfat yogurt with 1 tsp. no-sugar, all-fruit jam	70	0
Dinner:		
3 oz. shrimp or scallops, stir-fried in 1 tsp. sesame oil with 2 cups carrots, broccoli, red pepper and mushrooms	250	6
1 cup chicken broth with dash sherry and 2 very thinly sliced mushrooms	25	0
Snack:		
½ cup Anti-Cellulite Smoothie (diet p. 33)	50	0
TOTAL:	1075	14 (12% fat)

DAY FIVE

	Calories	Fat Grams
Breakfast:		
1 oz. lite cheese melted on	50	2
1 slice toasted whole-wheat bread	70	1
½ cup grapefruit juice	40	0
Snack:		
½ cup skim milk	45	0
Lunch:		
¾ cup Anti-Cellulite Tuna Salad (diet p. 30) stuffed in tomato on greens with ½ orange garnish	245	3
1 cup vegetable broth	20	0
2 *Fig Newtons* **or** 10 oz. no-salt	110	2
pretzels	110	1

	Calories	Fat Grams
Snack:		
1 Anti-Cellulite Bar (p. 128) **or** 6 cups air-popped popcorn	145	1
Dinner:		
1 cup pasta with 1 lean meatball (2 oz.) and 4 oz. Ragú sauce **or** 1 serving Lasagna (p. 148)	330	10
1 cup tossed greens with 1 Tbsp. no-oil dressing	20	0
1 poached pear	50	0
Snack:		
1 med. apple	80	0
TOTAL:	1205	19
		(14% fat)

DAY SIX

Once again it's time for a treat! 100 calories and 5
grams of fat! Remember a 4-oz. glass of wine, 2 small
cookies, 3 caramels, 10 peanut *M&M's*, ⅓ of a
Hershey's chocolate bar (1.65-oz. only) **or** a Weight
Watchers ice-cream sandwich.

	Calories	Fat Grams
Breakfast:		
Trail Mix made with 1 cup *Bran Chex*, 2 Tbsp. raisins, 10 no-salt pretzel sticks, 1 chopped apricot **or** 2 slices rye bread	180	0
½ grapefruit	40	0
Snack:		
1 fig	50	0
Lunch:		
1 10¾-oz. can low-sodium vegetable soup	160	4
1 cup tossed green salad with no-oil dressing	20	0
4 Kavli crackers **or** 6 Melba rounds	60	0

	Calories	Fat Grams
Snack:		
½ cup nonfat yogurt with 1 tsp. raisins	70	0
Dinner:		
Pita Pizza with 2 rinsed canned artichoke hearts, ½ cup each red pepper and mushrooms, 1 oz. part-skim mozzarella cheese and 2 oz. Red Sauce (p. 148) or Ragú sauce	250	6
1 cup chicken broth with 1 tsp. peas	25	0
Snack:		
4 oz. Anti-Cellulite Smoothie (diet p. 33)	50	0
TOTAL:	905 (10% fat)	10
With special snack:	1005 (13.5% fat)	15

DAY SEVEN

	Calories	Fat Grams
Breakfast:		
3 Buckwheat (p. 129) **or** 2 small regular pancakes	195	3
1 Tbsp. no-sugar, all-fruit jam	40	0
¼ cantaloupe	50	0
Snack:		
½ cup orange juice **or** low-sodium V-8	55	0
Lunch:		
2 oz. lean ham **or** 2 slices whole-wheat bread w/ 2 tsp. mustard	210	3
1 cup tossed salad greens with no-oil dressing	20	0

	Calories	Fat Grams
Snack:		
Fruit kabob or ½ cup cantaloupe	50	0
Dinner:		
Beans and rice (1 cup cooked rice and	220	1
¾ cup canned/rinsed black beans)	180	1
½ baked acorn squash with 1 Tbsp. honey, nutmeg and a dash of cinnamon	115	0
2 slices tomato and onions in no-fat vinaigrette	25	0
Snack:		
½ cup skim milk or Smoothie (diet p. 33)	45	0
TOTAL:	1205	8
		(6% fat)

WEEK THREE

DAY ONE

	Calories	Fat Grams

Breakfast:

¾ cup *Nutri-Grain* or any whole-wheat flake cereal	100	0
2 Tbsp. raisins	50	0
½ cup skim milk	45	0
2 tablespoons nonfat plain yogurt (served on cereal)	15	0

Snack:

1 fruit (orange, 15 grapes)	60	0

Lunch:

4 oz. Honey Spiced Fish (p. 142) **or** 4 ounces of any white fish (baked or broiled)	180	2
1 med. baked potato	110	0
2 oz. Potato Spread (p. 159) **or** 2 Tbsp. mustard	40	0
1 cup steamed broccoli	50	0

	Calories	Fat Grams
Snack:		
1 rice cake with	35	0
2 Tbsp. homemade Apple Butter (p. 160) **or** 1 Tbsp. regular apple butter	30	0
Dinner:		
1½ cups Spicy Split-Pea Soup (p. 134) **or** 1 cup kidney beans with ½ cup chopped green pepper & carrots marinated in 2 Tbsp. no-fat Italian dressing	230	2
1 slice whole-wheat bread	70	1
1 tsp. butter	35	4
Snack:		
1 Anti-Cellulite Smoothie (diet p. 33) **or** ½ cup nonfat yogurt	50	0
TOTAL:	1100	9
		(7% fat)

DAY TWO

	Calories	Fat Grams
Breakfast:		
1 slice of Basil & Tomato Quiche (p. 144) or 3 Egg-White Omelet (diet p. 40) with 1 oz. low-fat cheese and ½ cup vegetables	115	4.5
½ cup fresh orange juice	55	0
Snack:		
1 Anti-Cellulite Bar (p. 128) **or** ½ small banana and 2 graham cracker squares	145	1
Lunch:		
3 oz. turkey **or** chicken breast in whole-wheat pita with lettuce and 2 slices tomato, sprouts and 1 Tbsp. nonfat ranch dressing	280	4
1 med. apple	80	0

	Calories	Fat Grams
Snack:		
½ cup nonfat yogurt with 1 tsp. all-fruit jam	70	0
Dinner:		
1½ cups Caribbean Rice (p. 149) **or** 1 cup cooked brown rice, sautéed with 1 egg (**or** 2 oz. lean pork or Canadian bacon), 2 Tbsp. chopped green onion, ¼ cup julienne carrots, ½ cup green peas	385	6.5
¾ cup Szechuan String Beans (p. 154) **or** 1½ cups green beans	55	1.5
Snack:		
1 fig	50	0
TOTAL:	1235	17.5
		(12.5% fat)

DAY THREE

	Calories	Fat Grams
Breakfast:		
1 Lender's raisin bagel **or** ⅔ Sara Lee	165	1
1-oz. wedge low-fat cheese	45	3
½ grapefruit	40	0
Snack:		
1 oz (2 Tbsp.) raisins **or** 10 cherries	50	0
Lunch:		
½ cantaloupe with	95	0
1 cup 1% cottage cheese	160	3
½ cup strawberries	20	0
Snack:		
3 cups air-popped popcorn **or** 5 unsalted Saltines	70	1

	Calories	Fat Grams
Dinner:		
4 oz. Raspberry Chicken (p. 138) **or** 4 oz. chicken baked with a mixture of 1 Tbsp. Dijon mustard, 1 Tbsp. sherry, 2 Tbsp. water and herbs and capers	150	3
½ cup cooked wild rice	85	1
1 cup salad greens with nonfat dressing	20	0
6 spears steamed asparagus	20	0
Snack:		
½ cup skim milk	45	0
2 *Fig Newtons* **or** 1 ounce whole-wheat cereal with 1 tsp. raisins	110	2
TOTAL:	1075	14
		(12% fat)

DAY FOUR

	Calories	Fat Grams
Breakfast:		
1 English muffin with 1 tablespoon apple butter	175	1
½ cup grapefruit juice	40	0
Snack:		
1 cup skim milk	90	0
Lunch:		
3 oz. (roughly 15 med.) peeled shrimp with 4 ounces cocktail sauce	105 55	1 0
2 cups raw vegetables (carrots, broccoli, cauliflower, green and red pepper)	80	0
2 oz. Veg Dip (diet p. 36)	20	0

	Calories	Fat Grams
Snack:		
1 Anti-Cellulite Bar (p. 128) **or** 1 commercial nonfat fruit **or** bran muffin	145	1
Dinner:		
1 cup cooked rigatoni with 4 oz. Red Sauce (p. 148) **or** Ragú sauce, ¼ cup part-skim ricotta cheese, ½ cup steamed, chopped, drained spinach, and 1 Tbsp. fresh chopped basil, pinch black pepper	295	6
1 cup salad greens with nonfat dressing	20	0
1 cup steamed zucchini with oregano	25	0
Snack:		
½ cup Simplesse "fake fat" ice cream	120	0
TOTAL:	1170	9
		(7% fat)

DAY FIVE

	Calories	Fat Grams
Breakfast:		
1 cup oatmeal w/ cinnamon & 1 tsp. raisins	165	2
½ cup skim milk	45	0
½ cup unsweetened applesauce	50	0
Snack:		
1 med. orange	60	0
Lunch:		
BLT with 2 slices Canadian bacon on 2 slices whole-wheat bread, 2 slices tomato, lettuce and 1 Tbsp. light mayonnaise	265	7
1 apple	80	0

	Calories	Fat Grams
Snack:		
1 whole-wheat muffin (p. 130) **or** 1 cup skim milk	90	1
Dinner:		
Stuffed Onions (p. 155) **or** 3 cups mixed vegetables (onions, broccoli, snow peas, carrots) stir-fried in 1 tsp. sesame oil	210	5
¾ cup Caribbean Rice (p. 149) **or** 1 cup brown rice	195	3
½ cup brussels sprouts	30	0
Snack:		
1 Anti-Cellulite Smoothie (diet p. 33) **or** 2 Tbsp. raisins	50	0
TOTAL:	1240	18
	(13% fat)	

DAY SIX

Once again it's time for a treat! 100 calories and 5 grams of fat! Remember a 4-oz. glass of wine, 2 small cookies, 3 caramels, 10 peanut *M&M's,* ⅓ of a Hershey's chocolate bar (1.65-oz. only) **or** ⅔ Weight Watchers ice-cream sandwich.

	Calories	Fat Grams
Breakfast:		
1 whole-wheat muffin (p. 130) **or** 1 slice whole-wheat toast with 1 tsp. all-fruit jam	90	1
½ cup strawberries	20	0
Snack:		
1 banana **or** 1 med. papaya (105 calories)	110	0
Lunch:		
1 cup Shrimp Salad (p. 151) in pita with sliced tomato **or** Big Salad (diet p. 34)	350	5
1 med. orange	60	0

	Calories	Fat Grams
Snack:		
½ cup nonfat yogurt w/ 1 tsp. raisins	70	0
Dinner:		
Bean Spread (p. 159) in Burrito (heat wheat tortilla until warm, add ½ cup bean spread in middle. Sprinkle lettuce and chopped tomato, chopped onion to taste)	225	2
½ cup Guacamole (p. 136)	100	1
½ cup Salsa (p. 135) **or** Potato, Tomato and String Bean Special (diet p. 41)	35	0
Snack:		
3 oz. nonfat frozen yogurt **or** 1 cup nonfat plain yogurt	105	0
TOTAL:	1165	9
		(7% fat)
With special snack:	1265	14
		(11% fat)

DAY SEVEN

	Calories	Fat Grams
Breakfast:		
1 Anti-Cellulite Bar (p. 128) **or** ¾ English muffin and 2 tsp. honey	145	1
½ grapefruit	40	0
Snack:		
1 cup nonfat yogurt	110	0
½ cup blueberries	40	0
Lunch:		
Turkey, Pasta, and Vegetable Salad (p. 153) **or** 2 ounces turkey with 1 ounce low-fat cheese in whole-wheat pita with lettuce, tomato, sprouts, 1 Tbsp. honey mustard	285	7
1 oz. (2 Tbsp.) raisins	50	0

	Calories	Fat Grams
Snack:		
1-oz. wedge low-fat cheese and 2 Melba rounds	75	3
Dinner:		
4 oz. salmon basted with a mixture of 1 Tbsp. Dijon mustard, 1 Tbsp. honey, 1 Tbsp. balsamic vinegar and ½ tsp. minced garlic, baked for 5 minutes at 500 degrees **or** 4 oz. baked, broiled or grilled swordfish or trout	240	8
1 baked med. potato	110	0
2 oz. Potato Spread (p. 159) or 2 Tbsp. mustard	30	0
1 cup cooked carrots mixed with ½ Tbsp. fresh or ½ tsp. dry mint and ½ Tbsp. honey	80	0
Snack:		
4 oz. of Smoothie (diet p. 33)	50	0
TOTAL:	1255 (13.5% fat)	19

WEEK FOUR

DAY ONE

	Calories	Fat Grams
Breakfast:		
1 oz. Shredded Wheat	90	0
½ cup skim milk	45	0
1 tsp. honey	20	0
½ banana	55	0
Snack:		
½ cup raspberries **or** ½ orange	30	0
Lunch:		
2 asparagus rolls (roll 2 slices whole-wheat bread with rolling pin, spread ½ tsp. butter on each slice, add 2 asparagus stalks to each and roll up)	190	6
¾ cup Spicy Split-Pea Soup (p. 134) **or** 1¼ cups canned low-sodium minestrone	110	1
1 med. apple	80	0

	Calories	Fat Grams
Snack:		
2 Kavli crackers with 1-oz. wedge	30	0
cheese	45	3
Dinner:		
3½ oz. roast lean ham	180	9
Potato, Tomato and String Bean	205	5
Special (diet p. 41)		
1 cup cooked cabbage	30	0
Snack:		
Virgin Mary (1 cup tomato juice,	50	0
wedge lime, stalk celery, 2 dashes		
Tabasco)		
1-oz. wedge low-fat cheese in 1	50	3
celery stalk		
TOTAL:	1210	27
		(20% fat)

DAY TWO

	Calories	Fat Grams
Breakfast:		
1 oz. (1 heaping cup) Puffed Wheat cereal	105	0
½ cup skim milk	45	0
1 tsp. honey	20	0
½ med. banana	55	0
Snack:		
1 whole-wheat muffin (p. 130) **or** 1 med. apple (80 calories)	90	1
Lunch:		
4 oz. Salmon Pâté (p. 134) **or** 4 oz. canned salmon with 2 Tbsp. Pritikin or other nonfat Russian dressing	180	8
4 Akmak **or** 6 Kavli crackers	90	1
½ cup strawberries	20	0
Snack:		
1 orange	60	0

	Calories	Fat Grams
Dinner:		
1½ cups Navy Bean Soup with Asparagus (p. 133) **or** ¾ cup cooked wild rice mixed with 1 finely chopped medium cooked carrot, ½ cup diced cooked asparagus, ¾ cup chopped tomato, ½ cup each chopped celery and onion, 2 Tbsp. scallions, 2 Tbsp. lemon juice, 2 Tbsp. balsamic vinegar, ½ tsp. pepper, 1 minced garlic clove. Toss well. Chill.	230	2
Hot Spinach Salad (p. 150) **or** 2 cups raw spinach with 2 chopped cooked egg whites, 2 tsp. olive oil, 1 Tbsp. vinegar, ¼ cup garbanzo beans, ¼ cup sliced onion, ¼ cup sprouts (8 grams of fat)	185	7
Snack:		
½ cup Pumpkin Pie (p. 162) **or** 1 cup cantaloupe	60	0
TOTAL:	1140	19 (15% fat)

DAY THREE

	Calories	Fat Grams
Breakfast:		
½ cup Hot Wheat-Bran Cereal (p. 130) **or** 1 slice whole-wheat bread	70	1
1 banana	110	0
Snack:		
1 cup skim milk **or** 2 kiwifruits	90	0
Lunch:		
Big Salad (diet p. 34)	380	6
¼ cup low-sodium canned kidney beans with julienne carrot strips in 1 Tbsp. nonfat Italian dressing	130	0

	Calories	*Fat Grams*
Snack:		
1 oz. string cheese	70	5
Dinner:		
4 oz. Dijon chicken (diet p. 61) **or** 4 ounces grilled chicken	150	3
½ cup Sweet Potato Puree (p. 157) **or** 1 medium baked potato with 2 Tbsp. mustard	140	0
1 cup steamed broccoli	25	0
Snack:		
Smoothie (diet p. 33) **or** ½ pear	50	0
TOTAL:	1215	15
		(11% fat)

DAY FOUR

	Calories	Fat Grams
Breakfast:		
1 oz. low-fat cheese melted on whole-wheat toast	120	3
1 orange	60	0
Snack:		
1 Anti-Cellulite Bar (p. 128) **or** ¾ cup 1% cottage cheese with ¼ cup unsweetened applesauce	145	1
Lunch:		
1 cup Chicken Salad (p. 152) **or** 1 frozen croissant with 2 ounces chicken with lettuce, tomato, 1 Tbsp. "no fat" ranch dressing	270	8
6 Melba rounds **or** 4 Kavli crackers	60	0

	Calories	Fat Grams

Snack:

1 cup nonfat vanilla yogurt	125	0

Dinner:

2 Stuffed Zucchini (p. 156) with Red Sauce (p. 148) **or** 4 oz. Ragú sauce **or** 1 cup manhattan clam chowder with 2 slices whole-wheat bread with ½ tsp. butter or margarine ½ cup grapes (add 20 calories)	300	4.5

Snack:

2 figs	100	0
TOTAL:	1180	16.5
		(12.5% fat)

DAY FIVE

	Calories	Fat Grams
Breakfast:		
3 Egg-White Omelet (diet p. 40)	60	0
1 slice whole-wheat bread	70	1
1 tsp. butter or margarine	35	4
Snack:		
1 banana	110	0
Lunch:		
2 oz. turkey pastrami on 2 slices whole-wheat bread with 1 Tbsp. mustard	220	4
1 orange	60	0

	Calories	Fat Grams
Snack:		
3 cups air-popped popcorn	70	1
Dinner:		
1 cup salad greens with 1 Tbsp. nonfat dressing	20	0
1 piece Lasagna (p. 148) or 1 small fast-food plain hamburger	330	10
Snack:		
8 oz. Smoothie (diet p. 33) **or** Apple Blueberry Raisin Crisp (p. 165)	100	2
TOTAL:	1075	22 (18% fat)

DAY SIX

Once again it's time for a treat! 100 calories and 5
grams of fat! Remember a 4-oz. glass of wine, 2 small
cookies, 3 caramels, 10 peanut *M&M's*, ⅓ of a
Hershey's chocolate bar (1.65-oz. only) **or** ⅔ Weight
Watchers ice-cream sandwich.

	Calories	Fat Grams
Breakfast:		
1 cup nonfat yogurt with ½ cup blueberries	150	0
Snack:		
Banana Bread (p. 131) **or** 2 oz. raisins	120	2.5
Lunch:		
Anti-Cellulite Tuna Salad (diet p. 30)	245	3
Snack:		
Sparkling cranberry juice (4 ounces cranberry juice and 4 ounces sparkling water)	75	0

	Calories	Fat Grams
Dinner:		
2 oz. Pesto (p. 158) with 1 cup	100	7
cooked pasta **or** 1 cup pasta with 2	160	1
teaspoons olive oil (8 fat grams),		
½ tsp. garlic, 1 Tbsp. fresh basil,		
1 Tbsp. Parmesan cheese, pepper		
Angel Food Cake (p. 162) with	140	0
Strawberry Topping (p. 161) **or**	50	0
2 whole-wheat muffins (p. 130)		

Snack:	Calories	Fat Grams
½ cup frozen yogurt	105	0
TOTAL:	1145	13.5
	(10.5% fat)	
With special snack:	1245	18.5
	(13% fat)	

DAY SEVEN

	Calories	Fat Grams
Breakfast:		
French toast (dip 1 slice whole-wheat bread in 4 egg whites, add cinnamon, spray nonstick pan with Pam); top with 2 Tbsp. lite syrup	135	1
1 orange	60	0
Snack:		
1-oz. wedge Laughing Cow cheese in 1 celery stalk	55	3
Lunch:		
2 oz. Turkey in Lender's bagel with 1 oz. low-fat cheese, shredded lettuce, 2 slices tomato, and 1 Tbsp. light Italian dressing	325	5
1 tangerine	40	0

	Calories	Fat Grams

Snack:

| 1 Anti-Cellulite Bar (p. 128) **or** 10 flavored mini rice cakes | 145 | 1 |

Dinner:

| Fresh Fish Fillet with Veggies (p. 140) **or** 4 oz. broiled white fish with 2 cups mixed vegetables | 220 | 2.5 |
| 1 medium potato with 2 Tbsp. mustard | 135 | 0 |

Snack:

| Smoothie (p. 33) | 50 | 0 |
| TOTAL: | 1165 | 12.5 (9.5% fat) |

FOUR

THE MAINTENANCE FACTOR
How to Stay Slim, Dine Out and Enjoy Life!

SUGGESTED MAINTENANCE BY
DAILY CALORIE LEVEL

Now that you have been following the diet, you should be feeling trimmer and sleeker and have a positive sense of well-being. You may also be tempted to relax back into your old bad habits: you know, a chocolate-chip cookie here, some French fries there. If you continue to keep track of your fat grams and total calories, you'll be fine. But if you start overeating again you will not be feeling as terrific in the future.

This is the time to establish good habits and a solid maintenance plan that will keep you slim and happy. First of all, you should continue to eat regular, small meals instead of large ones spaced hours apart. You want to avoid that weak, grumpy feeling that comes during the long stretch between meals. That's a prescription for trouble! And you want to rely on what we call the 2–3–4–4 plan. This means that each day you have two servings of protein, three of dairy foods, four of whole grain products (breads, pastas or rice) and at least four of fruits and vegetables.

FIND YOUR NEW FAT-GRAM ALLOWANCE

For many people, knowing the right, nutritious foods to eat is the easy part. What is difficult is avoiding the "extras"—that scoop of ice cream or handful of peanuts. You have learned in previous chapters that you don't have to give up these things completely, as long as you monitor the fat grams in your diet. On the Anti-Cellulite Diet itself, you were eating about 15 grams of fat a day; on the maintenance phase, you can safely increase that figure.

To find the number of fat grams you may have each day during the maintenance phase, simply figure the percentage of your caloric intake as follows: multiply the number of calories you eat daily by .20 and divide that figure by 9. This equals your daily fat-gram allowance. For example, if you are a 130-pound woman eating about 1,300 calories a day and want to keep the percentage of fat in your diet at 20 percent, just multiply 1,300 $\times$ .20 to get the total fat calories of 260. Divide that by 9 (the number of calories in a gram of fat). This equals 29 fat grams.

Now, turn to the fat-gram chart in Chapter 9. Familiarize yourself with the fat content of foods you like. Also, look at the food-substitution list in Chapter 9 so that you will know how to swap low-fat foods for high ones. Gradually, all this will become second nature, just as counting calories was once part of your everyday life. But don't drive yourself crazy! Remember: you are the master of your own diet and not vice versa.

All this talk about fat grams does not mean that you can kiss calorie counting good-bye. A calorie is a basic unit of measurement and one pound of fat equals 3,500 calories. To lose one pound of fat, you have to reduce your diet by 3,500 calories. (By simply cutting 500 calories a day, you will achieve your goal.)

You now know that it is far easier to lose that pound when you reduce your fat intake. Nevertheless, that pound still has to go! So, here's yet another set of calculations:

LEARN YOUR BASIC CALORIE NEEDS

We don't all burn calories in the same way. If you and a friend went on the Anti-Cellulite Diet at the same time, one of you may have lost weight faster. This is because of several variables, including your genetic makeup, lean-to-fat ratio and level of activity. The genetic component is even more important than scientists previously thought. Studies have shown that when a group of people were kept in a strictly controlled situation, given exactly the same food and told to exercise in exactly the same manner, some lost several pounds more than others.

One reason for this is because we all have different metabolic rates. To find your basal metabolic rate (BMR), the number of calories your body burns at rest, multiply your current weight by ten. Then add more calories depending on your daily activity level. For example, if you weigh 130 pounds, your BMR equals 130×10. So, it takes 1,300 calories to sustain your body at rest. If you are a sedentary person (you have a desk job and no regular exercise program), multiply that number by .30 and add it to your BMR calories to get the total number of calories you personally require.

1. BMR = $130 \times 10 = 1,300$.
2. $1,300 \times .30 = 390$
3. $1,300 + 390 = 1,690$ calories for BMR + daily activities

If you are moderately active (you have a desk job, but exercise two to three hours per week or have a physically active job and no regular exercise program), you would multiply your BMR by .35; if you are constantly in motion and exercise three to five hours per week), multiply your BMR by .40.

CREATE A NEGATIVE ENERGY BALANCE

Here's what we call creating a positive out of a negative. Suppose you weigh 130 pounds and want to lose weight. You would then subtract 500 calories a day from the number of calories you need for your BMR plus daily activities to create a negative energy balance of 3,500 (500 $\times$ 7) calories a week. We're talking about losing real fat here, not just water. If you want to lose more weight, add exercise to the equation. So, you are creating a negative energy balance by eating less fat and calories and exercising more!

But don't go overboard. The Anti-Cellulite Diet itself fluctuates between 1,000 and 1,300 calories a day. On the maintenance phase, you should plan on eating between 1,300 and 1,800 calories a day, depending on your individual needs.

TAILOR YOUR OWN MAINTENANCE PLAN

Now is the time to devise your personal maintenance strategy using the guidelines and calculations in this book. Keep the basic Anti-Cellulite Diet as the core of your program and augment it with the extra fat grams and calories you are now allowed to have. You can add a few extra servings of bread, pasta, rice, nonfat desserts (see the recipes in Chapter 8), fresh fruits and vegetables, cereal or dairy products.

You should now know how to calculate the number of calories you may eat to maintain your new, slimmer weight. Find that number in the chart below. It will show you the right balance of various food groups to maintain your weight:

Calories	Protein (ounces)	Dairy (servings)	Fruit (servings)	Veg (servings)	Starch (servings)	Fat (servings)
1000**	4	2*	2	3	4	.5 tsp.
1200**	4	3	3	3	4	1 tsp.
1500	5	3	4	4	6	1.5 tsp.
1800	6	3	4	6	7	2 tsp.
2000	6	3	4	6	10	2 tsp.

* Take calcium supplement
** Take multivitamin capsule

EQUIVALENT LIST FOR 1,500 CALORIES

5 oz. Protein Equals: two 2–3-oz. portions of chicken, shellfish, meat, veal, fin fish or egg
Three Skim Dairy Product Servings Equal: one cup each of nonfat milk, nonfat yogurt, nonfat buttermilk
Four Fruit and Four Vegetable Servings Equal: choice of four fruits: one apple, ½ banana, 15 grapes, one cup berries, 2 tablespoons raisins, 4 oz. juice, one cup melon. Choice of four vegetables: two 1-cup servings raw, two ½-cup servings cooked
Six Starch Servings Equal: six of the following: one slice of whole-wheat or multigrain bread, ½ English muffin, ½ bagel, ½ pita, ½ cup pasta, ¾ cup flake cereal, ⅓ cup cooked rice, ½ cup corn or peas, or 2 rice cakes
One-and-a-Half Servings of Fat Equals: 1½ tsp. oil, 15 peanuts, 1½ tsp. butter or mayonnaise

THE POWER OF EXERCISE

By now you are in the habit of exercising regularly and have found the kind of workouts and sports that you really enjoy doing enough to keep on doing them. Exercise is the key to keeping weight off because it maintains that hard-earned lean body mass—the muscle that burns calories. Keep in mind that 75 percent of the calories you burn each day are used just to maintain your basal metabolism, which burns calories even as you sleep. And the only way to keep that basal metabolism high is by maintaining lean muscle mass through exercise.

Ideally, you should continue to burn 2,000 calories per week in low-to-moderate-intensity aerobic exercise. This could be as simple as taking a one-hour walk every day, jogging three miles or using a stationary bike thirty minutes a day or an hour every other day. Or you could burn those calories by taking a one-hour bench aerobics class three to four times a week. To vary your program, you will probably want to work out a cross-training plan that includes your favorite activities. For example, you might alternate swimming with running or cycling.

All the most recent research shows that among dieters, those who gain most of their weight back within one year are the ones who don't exercise throughout the diet and afterward. So even though they lose as much or nearly as much weight as dieters who exercise, they yo-yo right back to their original weight, and sometimes higher. Those who exercise, however, are more successful at keeping the weight off. Maintenance requires discipline; but not as much as dieting again and again. And you don't want to be right back where you started a year from now, do you?

WATCH OUT FOR THE FEAST-OR-FAMINE SYNDROME

Many dieters have an all-or-nothing approach to eating. They can starve themselves on liquid fasts all right, but then when they return to the day-to-day temptations of real life, they fall apart and overeat. So, it's important to get rid of that "I'm on a diet, I'm off a diet" mentality. Try thinking of the weight loss phase of the Anti-Cellulite Diet as Step One and the maintenance phase as Step Two. This phase requires as much discipline and thoughtfulness as you put into Step One, and possibly more. Are you up to the challenge? You've come this far, haven't you?

STRATEGIES FOR STAYING MOTIVATED

· Don't starve all day and then eat a big dinner. You'll be so hungry by then that you'll overeat. Besides, frequent, small meals throughout the day keep your metabolism revved up and running.
· Think of the people who love you and need you to be energetic and strong. Remember, you're not just doing this for vanity, you're doing it to take care of your health.
· Turn upcoming events into minigoals. "I've got to maintain this weight until Jeremy's birthday." And when the birthday is past, tell yourself, "I've got to make it to my school reunion looking good." It's the old "carrot before the horse"; but it works. Just take it one day at a time, and keep inventing new reasons to stay thin.
· Stay busy and don't let yourself get bored. Boredom makes you want to reach for a caloric quick fix. But

if you *do* feel bored, go to the gym, swim, play tennis—*anything* that makes you feel good. You'll forget about the boredom.

· Control anxiety with exercise, not chocolate. And if you need something to chew on to get you through anxious periods, make it sugar-free gum or air-popped popcorn.

· Schedule your workouts into your calendar each week along with all your other important appointments.

· Carry water or consommé with you in a bottle or Thermos throughout the day to prevent dehydration and fatigue. Now that the Thermos has become a chic fashion accessory, there are all kinds to buy.

· Keep an energizing snack handy—such as the Anti-Cellulite Bar—for those times when you need a mini-meal and there's nothing available except vending machines or junk food.

· Don't weigh yourself more than once a week so you don't have emotional reactions to the normal daily fluctuations of weight.

· Make an effort to substitute activity for food as the focus of your social life. Instead of planning a date for lunch or tea with a friend, invite her to go for a walk or even a jog. You'll be surprised at how welcome this change of pace will be to both of you. Or organize a bicycle trip instead of a barbecue to get your family and friends together for a day. The possibilities are endless—and lots of fun!

HOW TO SURVIVE DINING OUT

If you dine out frequently because of work, travel, social engagements or because you simply don't like to cook, you'll have to develop a strategy for ordering. Though restaurant chefs may not prepare food the same way you would at home, there are ways to deal with this. With practice, you can monitor how much fat goes into your body at a restaurant while still enjoying the meal and the occasion.

THE RESTAURANT RULE BOOK

1. Before dining out, eat a low-calorie snack to curb your appetite so you're not ravenous by the time you are served. If it helps, pretend you're Scarlett O'Hara, who ate before going to the picnic so she wouldn't disgrace herself with a greedy display of appetite once she got there. If you don't have a chance to snack beforehand, nibble on one small piece of bread and have a glass of water as soon as you sit down at the table.

2. Limit your alcohol before the meal. Sometimes, drinking before eating can increase one's appetite. Also, most people don't exert as much control over what they eat when they've had a drink or two. You're better off ordering mineral or soda water flavored with fresh lime, a dash of bitters or a splash of cranberry juice. A virgin mary or non-alcoholic beer are also good choices.

3. Watch out for the extras on the table: bread, butter, fried chips and noodles, which can add more fat and calories to your meal than the entree! Some taco chips are so loaded with fat that you can actually light them with a match and use them as candles.

4. Pay attention to the size of the portions! Remember a 3–5-ounce serving of protein is about the size of the palm of your hand and no thicker than the knuckle on your pinkie finger. A serving is not what a restaurant gives you, it's what *you* say it is. Sometimes you can ask

the waiter to put half the entree into a take-out bag right away or ask for a side plate and put a small individual portion on that to take home later. It can be easier to do this than to leave half of something you really like on your plate; and you know you can have it tomorrow. Better to store the remainder of dinner overnight in the refrigerator than over months on your thighs. Despite what we were told as children, it is not going to help the "starving children in China" if we scrape our plates clean; and besides, it is considered good manners to leave something on your plate.

5. Don't be afraid to ask for your food how *you* want it prepared. Choose broth or minestrone instead of a creamy soup. Order meats or fish broiled, vegetables steamed, potatoes baked instead of fried. Request all sauces and dressings on the side. Forget about sour cream, mustard tastes just fine on a potato. Little substitutions make a big difference in the amount of fat you eat.

6. Watch out for buffets—they are an invitation to overeat. If you are at a salad bar, avoid the creamy, mayonnaise-based selections and stock up on the greens, lean proteins and carbohydrates. Don't even *look* at those bacon bits, croutons and vegetables swimming in oil.

7. Splurge on a special occasion, but plan for it ahead of time by decreasing the fat in other meals that day. Sometimes, you *have* to indulge so you don't feel deprived. (Haven't you ever restrained yourself throughout a delicious dinner only to go home and raid the refrigerator?) Just don't make a habit of "special occasions" and eat less the days before and after.

8. Start dinner with a warm broth. This will decrease hunger pangs and help you feel fuller faster with less food. It takes twenty minutes to feel full and eating soup slowly before a meal gets you to the point of satiety

faster. Some people wolf down a hamburger in less than five minutes! Put the fork down between bites; sip water; take a few minutes to talk and enjoy the people around you. Don't just hurry through the meal.

9. Choose restaurants where you can have some control over what you are eating. An elegant French place that is proud of its traditional, sauce-laden cuisine may not take kindly to requests for fish or chicken broiled or grilled "dry," or sauce on the side. However, some sophisticated ones that cater to the expense-account set have grown accustomed to hearing these orders from their health-conscious regulars; they accommodate them gracefully. And your local bistro, where they know you and like you, will probably be glad to comply with your wishes as well. These days *everybody* understands being on a diet!

In selecting a restaurant, it's also important to know what kinds of menus are most complementary to the Anti-Cellulite Diet and maintenance plan. Here's a brief rundown of some ethnic cuisines:

Chinese. The good news is that Chinese cooking relies heavily on fresh vegetables, brown rice and noodles. The bad news is that Chinese chefs love loading their recipes with soy sauce, oil and monosodium glutamate (MSG). However, since most Chinese dishes are cooked to order, it's easy to tell the waiter, "No MSG and light on the oil and sauce, please." And avoid those wontons, rice and other fried dishes as well as egg rolls, crispy noodles, spareribs and the Pu Pu platters (found especially in the Hawaiian Islands), because they are all laden with fat. Instead, order wonton soup, steamed Peking rolls, steamed seafood and vegetables, roasted chicken or chop suey.

Japanese. Because the Japanese eat so much fresh seafood, vegetables and rice, they suffer far less heart disease than Americans. However, the Japanese do love salt, and this is what you have to watch out for at a Japanese restaurant. Order sushi or sashimi, and always make sure that you eat raw fish at a restaurant you know and trust. Ask the sushi chef what's fresh that day and watch to see if he keeps a clean work space and has continuous running water to wash the sushi board between orders.

If raw fish makes you nervous, order steamed dishes, salads with citrus vinegar, clear noodle soups and chicken or fish teriyaki with lots of vegetables. Limit your consumption of fried foods, smoked eel (high in fat), miso dressing (high in salt) or sake (alcohol).

French. Classic French cuisine is a real challenge for the dieter. Avoid the pâtés, the onion soup covered with cheese, the entrees smothered with Béarnaise or Mornay sauces. Ask instead for the simplest poached or grilled dishes on the menu or fish sautéed in wine. You can still request salad dressing on the side or just vinegar or lemon. Wave away the cheese course and the rich desserts and finish your meal with a compote of fresh fruit.

Seek out restaurants that offer nouvelle cuisine. Here the style of preparation is lighter. The emphasis is on simple grilled or poached fish and chicken and beautifully steamed baby vegetables. Nouvelle cuisine chefs prepare dishes enhanced with fruit and vegetable purees, herbs and wine instead of heavy sauces.

Italian. You have learned by now that pasta is included on the Anti-Cellulite Diet. So an Italian dinner can be a relaxing treat, as long as you remember the rules. Avoid those pastas with thick cream sauces (like fettuccine Alfredo) and pestos (loaded with pine nuts and cheese), or noodles filled with meat and cheese (like ravioli, cannelloni, manicotti and tortellini). Instead, select tomato and basil, primavera (vegetable), or marinara sauces. Pizza is also possible. Just order one with mushrooms, peppers, tomato or broccoli—not sausage, anchovies or pepperoni. Limit yourself to one or two slices. Many restaurants now offer cheeseless pizza, the best choice of all.

Tex-Mex. Problems as big as the Lone Star State itself begin the moment you sit down and eye that basket of fried and salted taco chips. Push this aside and ask for a toasted corn tortilla to dip in salsa (which is tasty and low in calories). Skip the margaritas—all that salt and tequila only makes you thirstier for another round. Try not to order entrees you know contain sour cream, cheese, chorizo sausage and guacamole. Fill up on gazpacho, black bean soup, chicken or bean burritos (sour cream on the side). Some other good options include sautéed shrimp in spicy sauce and *arroz con pollo* (chicken with rice).

While the ingredients in Tex-Mex food are basically healthy (corn, beans, vegetables and chilies), the quantities of sour cream and cooking oil can get you into trouble.

Dining out is one of the pleasures of life. There is no reason to give it up! All you have to do is control an evening out instead of letting it control you. Pick your restaurant carefully, order judiciously and forget the dictum: "Clean your plate!" You'll be fine.

FIVE

DIET Q & A

Candid Answers to Your Questions

Q: *I have to eat out for business luncheons. How do I stick to the diet?*

A: You can always order broiled fish or chicken, a baked potato or rice and a green salad; ask for dressing on the side. Or, order a fresh-fruit plate with one cup of low fat cottage cheese. Remember that your business clients are probably aware of health. Choose what you want without apology and urge your guests to order what they'd like.

Q: *After being on this diet for two weeks, I hit a plateau. What can I do?*

A: At some point, people stop losing pounds on the scale. What we don't like about the scale is that it doesn't truly reflect what's going on in the body. You may be building more muscle, which weighs more than fat. You may have *lost* fat and replaced the weight with muscle. This will eventually cause you to burn more calories and lose more weight. In other words, don't feel down, feel good because you are burning more calories, which will be better in the long run for weight loss.

Q: *I absolutely can't eat breakfast. What should I do?*

A: Have a piece of fruit or a slice of whole-wheat toast just to get something in your stomach. People who skip meals in the earlier part of the day tend to make up for it later, in the evening, the worst time of day to eat. If you're like most people, you're sedentary in the evening and will store fat if you eat a big meal or snack continuously. Make a big effort to eat breakfast.

Q: *Even though a high-fiber diet is supposed to relieve constipation, I find myself getting constipated anyway. How can I avoid this?*

A: Constipation *may* occur at first in people who aren't used to eating the amount of fiber in this diet. Drink plenty of water and keep exercising and your body will soon adjust.

Q: *I'm pregnant. How many calories should I add to your plan?*

A: No one should diet while they're pregnant. However, you shouldn't eat for two either! You can follow the maintenance program, but add 300 calories of extra dairy, whole grains and dark-green leafy vegetables.

Q: *Can my teenage daughter go on this diet?*

A: This is a healthy diet for *anyone,* although it is important for teenagers to get enough energy and nutrients for proper growth. Make sure that the calculations for calories and fat are adequate but low enough for slow, steady weight loss. (Refer to Chapter 3.) Young people can go on this plan because it will teach them better eating habits. Many teens eat too many calories from junk food. This diet is based on healthier choices with an occasional splurge.

Q: *I thought that you shouldn't eat red meat. Why is it in this diet?*

A: The key to eating red meat is to eat it in small amounts, not the 12-ounce steak at a steak house.

Lean red meat provides B vitamins, iron and zinc. Trimmed tenderloin of beef is a very lean choice. With a baked potato and vegetables, it makes a very healthy, balanced meal.

Q: *I like a glass of wine in the evenings. Can I drink during the losing phase?*

A: It's harder to nourish the body when you are getting a lower number of calories. If you add empty calories from alcohol, it's even harder to stay on a diet while still trying to nourish your body with healthier foods. Try to keep wine for a bonus treat. Don't let alcohol take the place of food. One 4-ounce glass of wine five days a week adds up to seven pounds a year!

Q: *Should I buy natural or synthetic vitamins?*

A: Both are considered equally effective.

Q: *I notice that some of the portions of cereal are 1 ounce or ¼ cup. Isn't that a small amount?*

A: A 1-ounce serving of some bran and granola types of cereal does seem slight, but adding some fresh or dried fruit or Puffed Wheat or Rice may make you feel as though you are eating more. You'll also notice that granola cereals are high in fat.

Q: *At times you give specific brand names. Does it really make a difference?*

A: Yes. Learn to read labels (see list p. 166). For example, spaghetti sauces can vary as much as 10 grams of fat per serving.

Q: *You permit extras like cookies and candy on special treat days. What is to stop me from bingeing on other days?*

A: We believe in the "out of sight, out of mind" principle. Keep the "bonus" treats behind other, healthier snacks in your cabinets and refrigerator. Put snacks like fruit, sliced vegetables, low-fat grain crackers, air-popped popcorn and nonfat dairy products in accessible places so you'll grab those first. Also, buy small packages of the treats so you won't be tempted to eat the whole thing.

Q: *I thought dried fruit was fattening. Why is there so much of it in your diet?*

A: While dried fruit *does* have more calories than raw fruit, the carbohydrate calories are not fattening when eaten in moderate amounts. Also, dried fruit provides quick energy and contains vital nutrients such as potassium, iron and fiber.

Q: *I like powdered creamer or real cream in my coffee. Will that add many calories?*

A: The calories from those creamers are almost 70 percent fat! There are 11 calories and .7 grams of fat in one teaspoon. Try evaporated skim milk instead.

Q: *What about "lite" foods?*

A: Read the label carefully. The terms "lite" or "light" do not always mean a product is lower in calories. For example, light olive oil means the color, not the calories or amount of fat. The government is working on labeling laws to set federal standards. In the meantime, be vigilant.

Q: *What oils should I use on this diet?*

A: While people talk about various oils being saturated, monounsaturated and polyunsaturated, the truth is that no oil contains any one type of fat, but a combination. Olive oil is 72 percent monounsaturated whereas cottonseed oil is 51 percent polyunsaturated but 26 percent saturated fat. The key is to choose those products low in saturated fats (olive, sesame and canola oils are good) and to eat small amounts of fats in general.

Diet Q & A

Q: *I love very rich ice cream. What can I do to satisfy this craving?*

A: Since some rich ice cream can contain 20 grams of fat per ½ cup, stay away from them completely. Instead, try frozen yogurt or the new "fake fat" ice creams, which taste just as good.

Q: *I like the taste of mayonnaise and I notice there is a lot of fat in a tablespoon of mayo. Is there anything I can substitute?*

A: Either find a low-calorie salad dressing or mix the mayo with nonfat yogurt. Remember, get the flavor without the fat!

Q: *How do I keep from raiding the fridge later in the evening?*

A: Hold yourself back for ten minutes and see if you are really hungry or it is just because you know the food is there. Go out for an evening stroll or play a card game to keep your mind off food!

Q: *There are some vegetables that I don't like that are included in this diet. What should I do?*

A: Look at the calories allotted and check the fat gram list in the back of the book for a substitute you do enjoy.

Q: *I like milk with my dinner, but I notice that you don't always allow it with a meal. What should I do?*

A: It is preferable to drink milk as a snack because calcium is absorbed most efficiently if eaten alone. However, if you want to save your dairy for dinner, do so.

Q: *You suggest four hours of low-intensity aerobics a week. How can I find that much time when I am a working mother?*

A: Of course, there are going to be days when you can't "get away" to exercise. But try to write exer-

101

cise into your daily schedule. With all the stress in your life, you'll *need* the endorphins released during exercise to help you cope! Endorphins are your own natural "feel good" chemicals.

Q: *I am a vegetarian and I don't eat meat or chicken, only fish. Can I be on your diet?*

A: Yes. The emphasis in this diet is on complex carbohydrates. Vegetarians should substitute protein-rich legumes and whole grains for meats and chicken. Remember, women need 46 grams of protein per day. Just watch how many calories you are getting from fat!

Q: *Do carbonated beverages such as diet soda or seltzer increase cellulite?*

A: This is an old wives' tale. We know of no research that supports this theory. However, regular carbonated sodas contain "empty" calories (with no nutritional value) and there is some evidence that diet sodas may increase your appetite.

SIX

THE EXERCISE FACTOR
What Works (and Doesn't!) to Fight Cellulite

WHY THE TORTOISE WINS THE RACE

Think of low-intensity aerobic exercise as the tortoise and anaerobic exercise—the kind that leaves you huffing and puffing and unable to carry on a conversation—as the hare. Aerobic exercise such as jogging for a half hour conditions the cardiovascular system by using steady, continuous movement that increases the body's use of oxygen over an extended period of time. Anaerobic activity—like quick one-minute sprints—doesn't use oxygen and is performed in intense bursts of energy. When it comes to burning fat and building muscle, it is definitely the tortoise that wins the race.

YO-YO GOT YOU ON A STRING?

According to research done at Stanford University, dieters who exercise regularly conserve their calorie-burning lean body mass, whereas those who merely diet lose significant lean body mass. This is why dieting without exercise can lower the number of calories you burn each day, leading to the "yo-yo" effect when you stop dieting and return to eating normally.

This explains the mystery of why:

- your super-slim friend can eat so much more than you do without gaining an ounce.
- the more you diet, the faster the weight comes back when you go back to eating normally
- two women who weigh the same on the scale can have such different-looking bodies and even wear different dress sizes.

In a word, it's—muscle!

As you now have learned, muscle is the major part of *lean body mass*—the "active" part of the body that burns calories—and fat is the inert "extra baggage" that does not. So your slimmer friend could be burning more calories because she has more lean muscle mass than you do. Muscle is also the reason why two women who weigh the same can wear different dress sizes. That's because, pound for pound, *muscle takes up only ⅕ as much space per pound as fat!*

And, there's only one way to both decrease body fat and increase lean muscle—exercise! As you become more fit, your body learns to use more body fat. If you eat fewer fat grams and burn more body fat through low-intensity aerobic exercise, you will see a smoother, sleeker and stronger body begin to emerge in a matter of weeks.

Not just any exercise will do this. It must be the right kind of exercise to eliminate cellulite—low-intensity aerobic exercise at 60 to 65 percent of your maximum heart rate. (See the chart on page 113 to find your individual working range.) Pushing your heart to a rate higher than 65 percent actually burns more glycogen (the body's readily available energy source) and a lower percentage of fat. And using up your glycogen stores can leave you feeling more worn out than invigorated. That's counterproductive.

Ideally, a woman should burn 2,000 calories per week in aerobic exercise of some kind. We recommend burning those calories with low-intensity low-impact aerobics. Though all levels of aerobic activity improve the cardiovascular system, the low range is preferable for burning fat and reducing the appearance of cellulite. And low-impact techniques accomplish this without the stress and injuries to the musculoskeletal system that can occur in high-impact aerobics. This program should be followed not only when dieting, but week in and week out throughout the year to maintain a healthy balance of nutrition and exercise.

Aerobic exercise is any activity that works large muscle groups to continuously maintain an elevated heart rate for fifteen minutes or longer, including aerobics, walking, biking, swimming, rowing, jumping rope, and cross-country skiing.

One important benefit of aerobic exercise is that it is the best way to get oxygen to your whole body. By breathing deeply during this kind of exercise, you achieve what exercise physiologists call "maximum oxygen consumption." This means your body obtains more oxygen at the cellular level. This increased availability of oxygen helps you burn more fat. Exercise also increases HDL (high-density lipoproteins, the "good" cholesterol) in your blood, helps control stress by releasing endorphins, the neurotransmitters in the brain that enhance your feelings of well-being; and adds to the overall *quality* and possibly even the *length* of your life.

To guide you toward these goals, we have gathered the latest information from universities, top research facilities and other medical and sports experts and created a streamlined state-of-the-art plan for maximum gain and no pain. The amount of time you need to burn 2,000 calories per week can be worked into even the busiest schedule because there are many ways to do it.

There's no wasted effort on this ultra-efficient program. You don't have to spend your life on a treadmill like some poor lab rat; low-intensity aerobic exercise is pleasant, as well as varied and not restricted to a gym. While it's a good idea to set aside time each day for an uninterrupted aerobic workout, you should look for ways to incorporate more activity into your daily life in an enjoyable way.

THE 3–3–3 FIT TRIPLE-THREAT ANTI-CELLULITE EXERCISE PLAN

The Triple-Threat Anti-Cellulite Exercise Plan is based on an easy-to-remember "3–3–3 FIT strategy. The 3–3–3 stands for: three goals, three ways, three times a week. FIT stands for: frequency, intensity and time—the key words for fitness.

Three Goals

1. To burn fat, not muscle.
2. To tone and contour the cellulite areas.
3. To reduce the stress that leads to overeating.

Three Ways to Proceed

1. Low-impact, low-intensity aerobics.
2. Muscle strengthening and toning exercises.
3. Adding more overall activity to your daily routine.

Three Times a Week

You will exercise a minimum of three times a week to burn that minimum 2,000 exercise calories per week.

THE BASIC FIT AEROBIC FORMULA

1. *Frequency:* MINIMUM 3 alternating days per week. Work up to five times if you like, but always take at least one day off a week.
2. *Intensity:* MINIMUM 60 percent of maximum heart rate and no more than 65 percent. Do not exceed this range or you'll burn less fat and more of the energy stores in your muscles. To burn fat go longer, not harder!
3. *Time:* MINIMUM thirty minutes of continuous aerobic activity. You may go as long as you can keep your heart rate within the 60–65 percent range, the longer, the better. Don't take your heart rate higher than 65 percent because this is a program for fat loss, not endurance training. But pace yourself intelligently so you don't work so hard at the start that you cannot continue the program. By working out on alternate days, your muscles have a chance to recover.

EXERCISE *CAN* MAKE THAT PEAR SHAPE MORE LIKE AN HOURGLASS

Strength training, such as working with weights, is a good addition to your basic aerobics program. It will help increase the size of muscle tissue and give more shape and contour to your figure. When shoulder pads came back into fashion, they proved a boon to the broad-hipped because they create the illusion of balanced proportion. But now that shoulder pads are on the way out again, you can use weight training to develop your upper body. Since most women have underdeveloped upper bodies, they will see significant improvement in just a few weeks when they start using weight training designed to strengthen that area. An added benefit of upper-body training is that it strengthens the neck and back and improves posture. Hence you appear taller and straighter and also move more gracefully.

Exercise can change the shape of your body only within the parameters of nature and proper diet. Some top models of the sixties had straight, boyish figures with no waistlines—and they carried this off so well that they made women shaped like Sophia Loren feel fat. No amount of exercise would ever give these models a classic hourglass figure, so they went with their strong point—with confidence. During the Renaissance, painters and poets idealized women with ample hips, bellies and thighs. Since most women are naturally shaped like that, it was easy to conform to fashion. Alas, in the nineties, women yearn to be tall, lean and athletic and want the narrow hips of an Olympic sprinter, the firm rounded bottom of the Girl from Ipanema and the high voluptuous breasts of a fifties movie goddess. Unfortunately, fewer than 5 percent of all women are born with even the *potential* for this body type. Even the fashion models who seem to be miracles of nature have in many cases sprouted their ample bosoms virtually overnight—with implants. Meanwhile, many women slave away, trying to achieve this impossible ideal and feeling inadequate because they don't look like the beauties in the *Sports Illustrated* swimsuit issue.

MAKE YOUR PERSONAL BEST YOUR GOAL

Look in the mirror and make a realistic appraisal of your body shape. Are you smaller on top than on the bottom? Do you have a curvy body but thin arms and legs? Are you boyishly straight-waisted? Hourglass curvy? Heavy-breasted? Short-legged? Broad-shouldered? Slope-shouldered?

These questions will give you an idea of what you can expect from your body and help you set goals to achieve your personal best. You can build up and contour weak and undersized arms, shoulders and legs with a weight-resistance program. You can reduce a great deal of that extra flab on the hips and thighs with weight loss, and firm it with exercise. You can make a small bust look much better with improved posture.

INACTIVITY, NOT AGE, IS TO BLAME FOR THAT DREADED MIDDLE-AGED SPREAD

As most people age they become less active and that's why they gain weight—not just because they're older. While most women acquire a larger percentage of fat with the years, some studies suggest it is *ideal* to always maintain the same body weight and lean/fat ratio that one has in their midtwenties. Regular exercise and a proper diet can definitely keep that ratio constant over the years and minimize the changes usually associated with aging.

IT'S NEVER TOO LATE TO BENEFIT FROM EXERCISE

The good news is that it's never too late to begin an exercise program. Studies at the Tufts University Center for Aging found that even people in their seventies gained muscle and stamina on a regular exercise program that included working with weights. Some felt so much better they even abandoned their canes and walkers.

EXERCISE KEEPS ON BURNING CALORIES EVEN AFTER YOU'VE STOPPED DOING IT

It is a mistaken assumption, but a common one, that the calories burned during exercise are the only ones to be used up as a result of that exercise session. You may think, for example, that in order to burn off one pound of fat (3,500 calories), you have to work out nearly twelve hours at 300 calories per hour. It looks like a pretty daunting task just to lose a few pounds by exercise. Fortunately, that is not the case because low-intensity exercise actually tunes up the metabolism and keeps it elevated for several hours after you have stopped exercising. For example, although a 130-pound woman burns only 300 calories during a relaxed one-hour walk, she will burn *more* calories in the hours *afterward* than if she had remained sedentary.

How Many Calories Can You Burn with Exercise?

The chart below shows how many calories a 130-pound woman will burn doing various aerobic exercises. These numbers are general estimates and vary depending on lean body mass and efficiency of technique.

Exercise	*Time in Minutes*			
	20	30	40	60
Aerobic Dancing (continuous)	200	300	400	600
Cycling (9.4 mph)	118	177	235	353
Jogging (10–12-min. mile)	193	290	386	579
Running (9-min. mile)	227	341	454	682
Swimming (continuous)	184	275	367	551
Walking (15–17-min. mile)	94	141	188	283

USE THE TABLE BELOW TO CALCULATE HOW MANY CALORIES *You* BURN

Simply find your weight range and multiply the caloric value given for one minute of activity by the number of minutes you perform the activity.

Activity	Weight in Pounds			
	105–115	127–137	160–170	181–192
Aerobic Dancing	5.83	6.58	7.83	8.58
Cycling (10 mph)	5.41	6.16	7.33	7.91
Jogging (5.5 mph)	8.58	9.75	11.50	12.66
Running (6.5 mph)	8.90	10.20	12.00	13.20
Rowing (easy)	3.91	4.50	5.25	5.83
Skiing (x-country 5 mph)	9.16	10.41	12.25	13.33
Stair-Climbing (normal)	5.90	6.70	7.90	8.80
Swimming (40 yds. per min.)	7.83	8.91	10.50	11.58
Walking (3 mph)	3.90	4.50	5.30	5.80

Adapted from Diet Free *by Dr. Charles T. Kuntzleman (Arbor Press, 1981)*

BURN FAT NOT ENERGY BY GOING THE DISTANCE

In the first twenty to thirty minutes of a workout, our bodies use up our glycogen stores and after that they begin to actually burn more fat. That's why it's important to work as long as possible at 60–65 percent of our maximum heart rate instead of in short bursts of great effort. If we are not fit, we build up lactic acid faster because oxygen is not getting to the muscles; this results in stiffness and soreness. Forget the old saying "No pain, no gain." It simply isn't true. And don't "go for the burn"; it just means you're pushing the muscle too hard. That can tear down muscle fiber, instead of strengthening it, and can result in soreness. As you proceed on the plan, your body's increasing ability to use oxygen enables you to lengthen your workout comfortably without fatigue.

Remember, it's more important to work longer at your correct heart rate than for a shorter time at a higher rate. Try to work up from twenty minutes every other day to thirty minutes or more, which will become increasingly easy to do as you advance with this program.

HOW TO FIND *YOUR* TARGET RATE ZONE FOR BURNING FAT

One of the keys to knowing if you're burning fat is to know if you're working your heart muscle in the target rate zone (60 to 65 percent of its maximum capacity) to produce a training effect. To find your heart rate:

- place your index finger lightly on the carotid artery on the side of your neck, or
- place your index and middle fingers on the radial artery on your inner wrist.

Then count the beats for exactly ten seconds and multiply that number by six.

As you exercise longer and/or more intensely, your heart rate goes up. Monitoring your heart rate at five-minute intervals is a good way to make sure you are exercising within your target zone. Start by taking your pulse five minutes into the workout (you should keep moving while doing this so that the heart rate remains elevated for continued aerobic benefits). *One rule of thumb; you should not be working so hard that you are too breathless to carry on a conversation comfortably.* After exercising, you should take your pulse again after the "cooldown" to make sure you've cooled down below 60 percent of your maximum heart rate. If you haven't, continue cooling down for a few more minutes.

HEART RATE TRAINING RANGES

Let's get started with finding your target heart rates on the chart below. First find your age and then refer to the heart rate numbers next to it to see if you are working in your target training range:

Age	60% Capacity	70% Capacity	85% Capacity	Maximum
20	120	140	170	200
25	117	137	166	195
30	114	133	162	190
35	111	130	157	185
40	108	126	153	180
45	105	123	149	175
50	102	119	145	170
55	99	116	140	165
60	96	112	136	160
65	93	109	132	155
70	90	105	128	150

THE FOUR BASIC PHASES
OF A GOOD WORKOUT

A good workout must include a warm-up, stretching, aerobics and a cool-down. Start by warming up for five minutes with slow, measured movements to prepare the body for exercise and reduce the risk of injury. Then stretch gently without bouncing *after* the muscles are warm. (Stretching cold muscles can tear them.) Now, proceed with the aerobic portion, which you should do continuously without stopping. When you're finished, cool down by *slowly* doing the same type of movements you've been doing, or just walking for two to three minutes. The blood tends to pool in the extremities after an intense workout and a cool-down lets the blood flow return to normal throughout the body and prevents fainting and undue stress to the heart. Then stretch again slowly to minimize the chance of waking up sore and stiff the next day.

WHY SPOT REDUCING DOESN'T WORK

What about spot-reducing exercises? Isn't that the way to get rid of that pesky padding? Spot exercises are very useful for toning the muscles for a shapelier look; but they do not burn the fat that covers those muscles. The stubborn weight in hips and thighs is the last to go because most women tend to lose fat from top to bottom. This is why diet and fat-burning low-to-moderate-intensity aerobics will work and spot-reducing exercises won't.

WHAT *DOES* WORK

Two of the newest innovations in low-intensity aerobics are the step-climber machines and bench aerobics. Both are designed to give a well-paced workout at whatever rate is best for you individually. They also protect the knee, leg and hip from the kinds of injuries that occur in high-impact exercise.

The step climber is something like stepping on bicycle pedals. You stand on two flat pedals and push down alternately with one foot while lifting the other. A moderate thirty-minute routine can provide a cardiovascular workout equal to jogging for a period longer than thirty minutes *without* the insult to your joints. Such a routine also helps tone muscles in buttocks, hips and legs. That's because continuously lifting the body's largest muscles against the force of gravity is hard work.

Bench aerobics—or step-ups—is the latest workout trend. This new approach, offered by gyms across the United States, combines the calorie-burning potential of climbing stairs with the energizing music and choreographed movements of aerobic dance. In bench classes you step on and off a sturdy bench 4–8 inches high, while coordinating a wide range of arm movements to a variety of steps. As "steppers" advance, they raise the height of their benches and add hand weights to increase the aerobic intensity and build muscle. Step training can accommodate out-of-shape beginners because the tempo is 120 beats per minute instead of the 150 beats in regular aerobics classes. Step-up classes are great for improving cardiovascular fitness while toning, tightening and strengthening the entire body, especially the hips, buttocks and thighs—those spots where cellulite is most prominent.

Traditional low-impact aerobics classes are also an excellent way to work out. Unlike jarring high-impact classes, in a low-impact session you keep one foot on the floor at all times, thus decreasing stress on bones, muscles and joints. Yet, you still burn fat and calories and get an overall solid workout.

Remember: Do the exercise that works best for you. If you enjoy it, you will keep doing it.

HOW TO CREATE A HOME MINI-GYM

If you don't belong to a health club or don't have access to a step-up class, you can set up an inviting mini-gym in your home. A good music system with your favorite sounds is a good motivator, and some flattering lighting is good, too. Another good source of motivation is an exercise videocassette. You can learn more about the full selection of fitness videos for aerobics, toning and stretching by calling 1-800-433-6769 to obtain a $2 catalog offering virtually everything on the market.

As for basic equipment, a stationary bicycle and a step-climber machine are two good options. Both tone the muscles in the hips, buttocks and legs while giving you a good (and safe) aerobic workout at whatever level of intensity you choose. You can even add a reading rack, available at most equipment stores, so you can enjoy a book or the morning paper as you work off the pounds. Step-climbers range in price from $60 to more than $3,000. Some have computerized instrument panels that display elapsed exercise time, stroke rate and total number of strokes. One new design works both upper- and lower-body muscle groups simultaneously with the addition of multi-position steel handlebars.

Stationary bicycles range from a few hundred dollars to thousands of dollars for models equipped with three-dimensional video screens that simulate a choice of thirty different ride courses (ranging from easy to difficult and including a choice of urban, desert or mountain scenery). Many bicycles are equipped with computers that help you monitor and program your training. For fat-burning purposes, we recommend that you avoid the hill-climbing programs and stick with a consistent, level pace.

Treadmills, rowers, recumbent bicycles and cross-country ski machines are also good for low-impact aerobic training.

Bench aerobics can be done in a home gym with one of the many step-bench videos now on the market. Bench Aerobix (800-252-3624) and The Step (800-729-7837) are mail-order sources that sell plastic benches and exercise videos you can use at home.

CROSS-TRAIN TO KEEP UP INTEREST

Remember, it's the regularity of fitness training, not just the intensity, that's the key to making and keeping your body at its best. So it's important to stay motivated and not make excuses. (Many people find it easier to exercise in the morning so that they don't find a way to put it aside as the day progresses.) The best way to burn 2,000 exercise calories per week without getting bored is by using a variety of activities. This is called cross-training. Here is an example of a one-week cross-training program that can be adapted to your needs, whether you're a beginner or an elite athlete.

A TYPICAL WEEK'S CROSS-TRAINING PLAN

Monday and Wednesday: Get on a bike and pedal around the neighborhood for forty-five minutes. Do five to ten minutes of calf stretches afterward so you won't get stiff.

Tuesday and Thursday: Work out on a step-climber at home or at the gym for a half-hour session each day.

Friday: Work out with light weights. Lunges and squats with light weights are an excellent way to firm and tone the thighs and derriere. You can learn how to use weights from a number of books and videos on the market; it's a good idea to consult a qualified staff member or trainer at your gym or some other exercise professional to make sure both your form and the weights are correct.

Weekend: Take a two-hour hike one day or a one-hour hike each day. The mountains or the beach are always nice; you may even want to take the time to explore a part of town. Hiking doesn't necessarily mean you have to tromp up peaks with a pack on your back. You can tromp through your neighborhood in a comfortable pair of walking shoes and get all the exercise benefits you need as long as you're maintaining a good aerobic pace.

Anaerobic activities like tennis, weight lifting, volleyball, waterskiing, downhill skiing, sprinting and other stop–go sports burn mainly glycogen (the energy stores in your muscle) quickly and without oxygen. You still burn calories, but your heart rate is not elevated continuously throughout the activity. So anaerobic workouts are good for muscle tone, but do not serve the same purpose as aerobic exercise. If you don't have enough time for both, the aerobic portion of your workout should take priority.

However, both aerobics and anaerobics contribute to a total exercise program; interspersing them lends variety and makes staying active more fun.

PUT MORE ACTIVITY INTO
YOUR DAILY ROUTINE

Relaxed exercise, such as taking a stroll, watering your garden or crawling around on the floor playing games with your children, not only raises your metabolism but reduces the anxiety, frustration and tension that cause many women to turn to food for solace and comfort. Emotional relief is as vital a part of a woman's health and fitness program as any diet or aerobics class. If you are

118

happy, you are more motivated to take good care of yourself.

GO ALL OUT FOR YOUR BEST POSSIBLE SELF

No body is infinitely malleable, not even with cosmetic surgery. The French women who have always been known for their great sense of chic have devised many clever strategies for making the most of less-than-perfect faces and figures; but the essence of their style is personal flair, confidence, poise and bearing. They've made an art of knowing how to distract attention from their flaws and focus it on their assets. Think about how you can do the same.

Most important, keep a clear perspective. Don't sacrifice living your life for a fanatical pursuit of the perfect body. Not only does this not work, but it often backfires; stress and feelings of deprivation often accompany obsessive behavior.

So do what top athletes do: don't think about the competition, just go all out to achieve your Personal Best.

And feel the satisfaction of being a winner!

SEVEN

TREATMENTS AND PRODUCTS
The Role of All Those Rubs, Wraps and
Anti-Cellulite Creams

WOULDN'T IT BE WONDERFUL to be able to just massage away that nasty cellulite with a magic potion?

You're not the only one who thinks so. In fact, this is such an appealing concept that it is the foundation of a multimillion-dollar international industry. Products, treatments and spa programs designed to banish cellulite suddenly seem to be turning up everywhere. Department stores are stocked with expensive and exotic product lines. Depending on how much you dislike your cellulite—and how much time and money you have to spend—this is just the beginning and the sky is the limit.

What works and what doesn't is a subject of controversy between the medical establishment and the purveyors of products and services. Currently, we know of no papers published in the medical journals to support the claims made by the cosmetic companies about cellulite.

CREAMS AND GELS

Throughout the United States, many products have become available at fashionable cosmetics counters. Clarins, Terme di Saturnia, Body Line, Elancyl, La Costa and

other companies all offer anti-cellulite products. Cellu-
lite-control gels are promoted as having slimming, firm-
ing, tightening and stabilizing properties; advertisers
promise that they will improve contours and end the
appearance of sponginess. Scientific-sounding ad copy
sings the praises of a dizzying array of ingredients, including bio-microspheres, butcher's-broom, seaweed
and various botanicals.

Do all these claims sound confusing?

Dermatologists generally believe that cosmetics do
not get under the skin and change cellulite. Nevertheless, the cosmetics companies and many who use their
products would argue that there are visible results. By
caring for your skin with *any* good cosmetic product, you
are helping to improve its surface appearance. An anti-
cellulite cream or gel may well make your skin look and
feel better on a short-term basis.

Keep in mind that anti-cellulite creams and treatments
are part of a more comprehensive program of taking care
of yourself. If a cream or gel makes your skin *feel* pampered, then go ahead and use it. However, remember the
bottom line: no cream or treatment works alone without
a far wider program of diet and exercise. It's what you
eat and how you exercise that contributes to your overall
health. Just keep things in perspective. Don't regard surface treatments as a panacea.

Heinz Eiermann, director of the Division of Color and
Cosmetics of the Food and Drug Administration, the
U.S. government regulatory agency for drugs and cosmetics, tries to put things in perspective: "When cosmetics companies are talking about 'firmness' and
'smoothness,' they are not talking about changing the fat
[cellulite] in your body or even beneath your skin; and
when they're talking about appearance, this is a physical
effect only."

SPA TREATMENTS

HERBAL WRAPS

Most spas offer an herbal-wrap treatment. You are swathed like a mummy in sheets dampened with an herbal brew and left to lie in a darkened room for a half hour or so. Advocates of herbal wraps say that they rid your body of impurities through perspiration in the same way as exercise. Some people believe you can just lie there and get thin without working out. That would be wonderful if it were true! But alas, there is no evidence to suggest that herbal wraps do any more for you than allow you to calm down and maybe get a good nap, which is, perhaps, the best anti-stress beauty treatment of all.

ALGAE WRAPS

You are slathered with a thin, silky full-body mask rich in minerals, cola (a plant extract) and ivy and algae extracts, then wrapped in silver foil to rest for a half hour or so. Proponents say that the treatment helps the body eliminate toxins by intensifying the natural perspiration of the skin; the contents of the mask are also said to interact with various skin components to stimulate the function of tissue regeneration and the reduction of cellulite.

MUD TREATMENTS

The principle of a mud treatment is similar to that of an algae wrap. However, instead of being covered with a mask formed from the sea, you are slathered with mineral-rich mud imported from volcanic areas of Italy. After you have rested for a half hour or so with your body encased in mud, you then head for the shower. Proponents of mud treatments say that their skin feels silky smooth for days afterward.

MASSAGE

Any type of massage, from the soothing Swedish style to the more aggressive Shiatsu, is good for relaxation and for stimulation of circulation; but there is one that practitioners claim is especially good for problem cellulite. It is called lymphatic drainage massage, so named because it is said to filtrate and refiltrate the lymph (white blood) cells. Practitioners of this lymphatic technique massage the body with a light, twisting motion, an approach developed by Dr. Emil Vodder, a Dane who practiced on the French Riviera. Vodder's treatment supposedly improved edema (swelling that comes from water retention) and bowel function. Vodder trained and licensed others to practice this special lymphatic massage, which is available at some of the world's most luxurious spas including the one at the Ritz Hotel in Paris; Cal-A-Vie in Vista, California; and the Marriott Desert Springs in Palm Springs, California. Though there is no medical evidence to support the theory that cellulite can be banished with lymphatic (or any other kind) of massage, these treatments can relax you and give you a sense of well-being.

HYDROTHERAPY

Hydrotherapy is massage with water, like a Jacuzzi. Spas offering hydrotherapy are often equipped with custommade tubs with multiple jets (some are computer-programmed); this treatment relaxes the body and supposedly improves circulation.

Hydrotherapy can also be done by a therapist using a handheld pressurized hose (sometimes called "The Scottish Hose").

For at-home hydrotherapy, the Windmere company manufactures a showerhead massager.

THALASSOTHERAPY

This is a course of treatments incorporating wraps and hydrotherapy. Plankton, sea algae, fresh dried seaweed and sea water are used in the treatment to relax and supposedly detoxify the body. For example, a hydrotherapy algae bath is a purifying bath in a deep European tub. Of the 25,000 different kinds of algae used in thalassotherapy, brown laminaria and focus algae are considered the most beneficial for the body. Europeans have been using algae from the coastline of Brittany since the 1800s for what they call "the Cure." However, it is only in the last decade or so that they have incorporated it into treatments specifically designed for cellulite.

SPECIAL SPA CELLULITE PROGRAMS

At spas in Europe and the United States, you can indulge in a week-long anti-cellulite program. A typical program at a spa in Brittany includes: algae baths or masks on alternate days; a regular half-hour exercise session in a pool equipped with pressure hoses aimed at cellulite areas; a half-hour daily regime on a machine like the stationary bicycle; weight machines that work the legs; an exercise regime using sticks and rolling balls; a therapy session in which you wear "moon boots" (pressurized waist-high balloon-like objects) that contract, supposedly improving lymphatic drainage; fifteen minutes in a "steam cabin"; and treatment with a high-pressure Swiss shower hose (manned by an attendant who aims water at cellulite areas). In addition, spa guests are put on a 1,000-calories-a-day diet to help the process along.

At spas all over Europe and the United States, there are similar regimes. Leading spas that attack cellulite with thalassotherapy and/or hydrotherapy in Europe include the Biotherm, the Deauville, Evian and the Grand Hotel at St. Malo in France; and Sturebadet in Stockholm, Sweden. Those in the United States that offer these treatments include the Doral Saturnia in Miami; the Claremont in San Francisco; Burton Creek in Austin, Texas; the Marriott Camelback in Scottsdale, Arizona; the Desert Springs Marriott near Palm Springs; and Cal-A-Vie in Vista, California.

LIPOSUCTION

Liposuction, which costs thousands of dollars, is a much more radical approach to eliminating unwanted bulges on hips, thighs, buttocks, stomachs and other places. Some women even use it for knees and ankles! However, it is far from being a panacea. Steven Hoefflin, M.D., the prominent Los Angeles plastic surgeon who has perfected the faces and bodies of many top Hollywood stars, cautions that liposuction is not perfect. "If someone wants their skin to be as smooth as an eighteen-year-old, it just won't happen," he says. He points out that as women age, their skin becomes looser, though the fibrous bands just beneath the skin do not. That's what creates the increasing appearance of cellulite as women age.

However, there is a new surgical technique being used by some specialists like Hoefflin to minimize the appearance of cellulite. Those fibrous bands are loosened before liposuction is performed. An incision is made with a narrow instrument about the width of a wire coat hanger outfitted with a V-shaped hook at the end. The physician maneuvers this hook beneath the fibrous bands to cut and loosen them and then smooths the area with a skin graft. Then he performs liposuction at a deeper level—not just beneath the skin but nearer the muscle. For some women, this can result in a much smoother appearance than the basic liposuction technique.

Liposuction involves all the risks of serious surgery, including general anesthesia; it should not be taken casually. There is a recovery period of about six weeks when the patient must wear an elastic garment to help the skin adhere properly, and must not be too physically active. Clearly, from everything you've learned in this book so far, that's pretty counterproductive to your goals.

SUMMING UP

Throughout this book, the emphasis is on adherence to a good healthful diet, with regular exercise, little or no alcohol and plenty of water every day.

There is where the real "magic" is! That is not to say, however, that it doesn't feel nice to be pampered. What woman doesn't look and feel better after setting aside some time to take care of herself? Whether it's simply massaging the skin with a comforting cream or spending a leisurely week at a spa, you are sure to feel better simply because you have paid attention to your own needs.

EIGHT

FORTY-FIVE RECIPES
That Are Low-Fat and Fun

Breakfast and Brunch

ANTI-CELLULITE BAR

1 1/2 cups Quaker Oats, dry
1 cup Puffed Wheat cereal
3 cups Puffed Rice cereal
1/2 cup raw wheat bran
1/2 cup frozen apple juice
   concentrate
1/3 cup honey
3 tablespoons light corn syrup
2 tablespoons molasses, black
   cane

1/2 cup raisins, firmly packed
4 ounces dried apricot, finely
   chopped
1 teaspoon ground cinnamon
2 tablespoons dried sesame
   seeds
Vegetable spray

Preheat oven to 275 degrees. Combine all ingredients
except sesame seeds in a large mixing bowl. Mix all ingredients thoroughly with a wooden spoon, starting
from the side of the bowl and making sure that all the
ingredients are combined. Mix for 5 minutes. (Good arm
workout!) Pour into a 10-by-10-inch or 9-by-11-inch vegetable-sprayed baking pan. Press mixture down completely into pan. Flatten by pushing the mixture down
strongly with a spatula. Top with sesame seeds, then
push down again. Bake at 275 degrees for 50 minutes to
1 hour. (Chewy texture at 50 minutes.) Remove from
oven and let cool slightly. Slice while still warm with a
very sharp knife into 5 columns and 3 rows, making 15
bars. Tastes great warm, but wrap individually in aluminum foil to preserve. These bars are preserved naturally
by all the juice; there is no added fat, which typically
oxidizes.

Keep some bars out for the next week of snacks, then put the rest in the freezer for long-term storage. They can be warmed up for breakfast or snack as needed!

YIELD: 15 bars

CALORIES: 145

FIBER: 3 grams

FAT GRAMS: 1

IRON: 2.5 mg.

CALCIUM: 38 mg.

CHOLESTEROL: 0

SODIUM: 10 mg.

6% FAT

Lots of potassium and vitamins for energy!

BUCKWHEAT PANCAKES

1 cup buckwheat flour
1 cup regular all-purpose flour
2 medium eggs
2 cups low-fat buttermilk

2 teaspoons baking powder
1 teaspoon baking soda
1 tablespoon molasses
Vegetable spray

Combine all ingredients in mixing bowl. Let sit for 10 minutes, then spray vegetable spray in pan or on griddle.

YIELD: 6 servings (3 pancakes each)

14% Fat

CALORIES FOR 3
   PANCAKES: 195

FAT GRAMS: 3

CALCIUM: 225 mg.

SODIUM: 347 mg.

FIBER: .5 grams

IRON: 1.5 mg.

CHOLESTEROL: 82 mg.

HOT WHEAT-BRAN CEREAL

¹/₄ cup raw wheat bran
1 teaspoon raisins
Pinch nutmeg

Pinch cinnamon
¹/₄ cup apple juice
¹/₄ cup water

Place the bran, raisins, nutmeg and cinnamon in a small bowl. Bring the apple juice and the water to a boil, and pour over the bran. Serve hot.

YIELD: 1 serving

SERVING SIZE: ¹/₂ cup
CALORIES: 70
FAT GRAMS: .7
CALCIUM: 24 mg.

SODIUM: 4 mg.
FIBER: 6.5 grams
IRON: 2.5 mg.
CHOLESTEROL: 0 mg.

Modified recipe of the Doral Saturnia International Spa Resort.

WHOLE-WHEAT MUFFINS

2 cups whole-wheat flaked
   cereal (Nutri-Grain,
   Wheaties, Total)
1 cup low-fat buttermilk
1 cup whole-wheat flour
³/₄ teaspoon baking soda
¹/₄ teaspoon ground cinnamon

¹/₂ cup diced apple
2 tablespoons raisins
¹/₄ cup unsweetened apple
   juice
¹/₄ cup molasses
1 egg
Vegetable spray

Preheat oven to 400 degrees. Spray 12 medium-sized muffin tins with vegetable spray. Pour buttermilk over cereal in bowl, let sit 5 minutes. Sift dry ingredients, add all remaining ingredients and mix with wooden spoon. Fill until each muffin tin is ³/₄ full. Bake for 20 minutes.

YIELD: 12 muffins

CALORIES: 90	FIBER: 2 grams
FAT GRAMS: 1	IRON: 3.5 mg.
CALCIUM: 68 mg.	CHOLESTEROL: 20 mg.
SODIUM: 124 mg.	

WHOLE-WHEAT BANANA BREAD

1/3 cup honey
2 tablespoons butter or
    margarine
1 teaspoon vanilla
1/4 teaspoon salt
2 cups very ripe bananas,
    mashed
2 tablespoons lemon juice
1 1/2 cups whole-wheat pastry
    flour

1/2 cup whole-wheat bread
    flour
2 teaspoons baking powder
1/2 teaspoon baking soda
1/2 cup dried dates, finely
    chopped
1/4 cup walnuts, chopped
Vegetable spray

Preheat oven to 350 degrees. Spray a bread pan (8 by 4 inches) with vegetable spray. Beat honey, butter or margarine, vanilla, and salt. Add banana and lemon juice. Sift flour, baking powder and soda. Mix all wet and dry ingredients together. Fold in dates and walnuts, reserving 1 tablespoon of nuts for top. Pour into bread pan and bake for 1 to 1 1/2 hours. Cool, then slice. Very moist bread.

YIELD: 18 slices

CALORIES: 120	FIBER: 1.6 grams
FAT GRAMS: 2.5	IRON: .3 mg.
CALCIUM: 34 mg.	CHOLESTEROL: 3 mg.
SODIUM: 103 mg.	

Soups and Starters

BUTTERNUT SQUASH SOUP

1 cup diced potatoes
3 cups raw butternut squash,
    peeled and seeded (easier
    to peel if boiled for 10
    minutes)
3 whole celery stalks
1 cup green apple, core
    removed (leave skin on)
1 large yellow onion, peeled
    and chopped

3 cups chicken stock or
    low-sodium chicken broth
2 sprigs fresh rosemary
2 sprigs fresh marjoram
1/4 teaspoon black pepper
1 teaspoon lemon juice
1 minced garlic clove

In a large saucepan, combine all ingredients. Bring to a boil, then simmer until everything is tender: about 30 minutes. Allow mixture to cool, then take out celery. Puree in a blender at high speed until smooth. (Be careful when blending hot food. The lid should be held down while the machine is running so soup does not suddenly explode and fly all over the kitchen.)

This soup can be frozen.

YIELD: 8 (3/4-cup servings)

SERVING SIZE: 3/4 cup or
    6 ounces
CALORIES: 55
FAT GRAMS: .5

CALCIUM: 20 mg.
SODIUM: 4 mg.
FIBER: 1 gram
CHOLESTEROL: 0

Modified from a recipe created by Michael McVay, formerly of the Doral Saturnia International Spa Resort.

NAVY-BEAN SOUP WITH ASPARAGUS

24 ounces (3 cups) dried navy
    beans
6 cups water (or 9 cups if no
    chicken broth)
3 cups chicken broth
1/2 pound lean cooked ham cut
    into 1/2-inch cubes (trim
    all fat)
3/4 pound asparagus stalks
    (reserve tops to add at
    last stage of cooking)

3 stalks celery, chopped
1/2 medium diced onion
1 chopped carrot
1 teaspoon white pepper
1/2 teaspoon paprika
1/4 teaspoon thyme
1 1/2 teaspoons cajun spice
2 bay leaves

Soak beans overnight. Rinse well. Discard any bad or floating beans. Combine all ingredients except asparagus and simmer for 2 hours. Add asparagus stalks and cook for about 15 minutes. Then add tops 5 minutes before serving.

YIELD: 25 (3/4-cup servings)

CALORIES: 115
FAT GRAMS: 1
CALCIUM: 49 mg.
SODIUM: 13 mg.

FIBER: 3 grams
CHOLESTEROL: 6 mg.
IRON: 2 mg.

SPICY SPLIT-PEA SOUP

1½ lbs. lean ham (½"
    thick)
15 cups chicken stock
3 cups dried split peas, soaked
    overnight in 9 cups water,
    cleaned and drained
2 bay leaves
1 cup chopped onion
1 cup finely chopped carrot
2 cups chopped celery
1 cup chopped potato
2 cloves chopped garlic
1 teaspoon thyme
1 teaspoon brown sugar
Pinch red pepper flakes
2 dashes Tabasco
Pinch cayenne

In the chicken stock, simmer peas with ham slice, trimmed of all fat, and bay leaves for 2½ hours. Then add onion, carrots, celery, potato, and all remaining ingredients. Simmer for ½ hour more to blend flavors. For a smooth consistency, you may want to run mixture through a blender or sieve.

Freeze and store in mini portions.

YIELD: 18 cups, or 24 (¾-cup) servings

CALORIES: 115
FAT GRAMS: 1
CALCIUM: 25 mg.
SODIUM: 18 mg.

FIBER: 1.7 grams
CHOLESTEROL: 0
IRON: 1.3 mg.

SALMON PÂTÉ

10 ounces low-sodium canned
    or fresh baked salmon
2 tablespoons low-calorie
    mayonnaise
3 ounces nonfat plain yogurt
¼ cup chopped purple onion
1 celery stalk, chopped
2 tablespoons Dijon mustard
1 teaspoon dill
1 ounce lemon juice

Combine all ingredients in a food processor or blender for 2 minutes. Mixture should be smooth. Chill, then serve.

YIELD: 16 1-ounce servings

CALORIES: 45

FIBER: 0

FAT GRAMS: 2

CHOLESTEROL: 10 mg.

CALCIUM: 14 mg.

IRON: .2 mg.

SODIUM: 52 mg.

SALSA

4 cups chopped peeled
   tomatoes, fresh or canned
3 tablespoons chopped cilantro
   (Chinese parsley), or 1
   tablespoon dried
1 cup onion, finely diced
1/4 cup chopped scallion
2 diced green chilies, canned
2 tablespoons tomato paste

1 teaspoon red wine vinegar
1 tablespoon lemon juice
4 cloves garlic (or 1 1/2
   teaspoons minced garlic or
   1 teaspoon powdered
   garlic)
2 dashes Tabasco
Pinch cayenne

Fresh tomatoes should be blanched in boiling water for 1 minute then cooled, peeled, and diced. Mix all ingredients and chill.

YIELD: 8 4-ounce servings

CALORIES: 35

FIBER: 1.2 grams

FAT GRAMS: 0

CHOLESTEROL: 0 mg.

CALCIUM: 20 mg.

IRON: 1 mg.

SODIUM: 1 mg.

GUACAMOLE

2 ripe avocados, mashed
1 cup plain nonfat yogurt
1 large tomato, diced (1½ cups)
1 small onion, chopped
2 tablespoons scallions, chopped
2 cloves garlic, chopped
3 green chilies, seeded and

minced (add more according to taste)
¼ cup fresh chopped coriander
1 cup salsa (recipe page 135)
¼ teaspoon cayenne
½ teaspoon ground cumin
Dash Tabasco
1½ tablespoons lemon juice

Combine all ingredients and chill. Serve with tacos, fajitas, enchiladas, or corn chips.

YIELD: 8 ½-cup servings or 32 1-ounce servings

CALORIES: 100
FAT GRAMS: 1.3
CALCIUM: 56.5 mg.
SODIUM: 24 mg.

FIBER: .4 grams
CHOLESTEROL: 0 mg.
IRON: .65 mg.

SALMON AND CAPER DIP

1 teaspoon olive oil
1/2 medium onion, chopped
2 cloves garlic, minced
4 green chilies
1 7-ounce can low-sodium
  salmon
2 tablespoons dry white wine

Pinch nutmeg
1/2 teaspoon dill
1 1/2 tablespoons parsley
2 teaspoons capers
4 ounces scallions, chopped
2 ounces nonfat yogurt
2 ounces light sour cream

Heat oil and sauté onion and garlic. Stir in carrots, chilies and salmon with liquid, cook for 10 more minutes. Add in all remaining ingredients except yogurt and sour cream. Cook 5 more minutes. Put mixture in blender with yogurt and sour cream. Blend, then chill for at least 2 hours.

YIELD: 12 1-ounce servings

CALORIES: 50
FAT GRAMS: 2
CALCIUM: 59 mg.
SODIUM: 57 mg.

FIBER: .4 grams
CHOLESTEROL: 1 mg.
IRON: .6 mg.

Entrees

RASPBERRY CHICKEN

2 whole skinless and boneless
    chicken breasts, 8 ounces
    each, pounded very thin
1/8 teaspoon black pepper
1 1/2 tablespoons red wine
    vinegar

2 ounces white wine
1/2 cup fresh or frozen
    raspberries
2 teaspoons butter or
    margarine
Vegetable spray

Sprinkle pepper onto chicken breasts. In a nonstick pan, spray vegetable spray and melt butter. Sauté chicken over medium heat until brown. Remove chicken and pour vinegar and wine into pan to deglaze. Stir in raspberries and cook over high heat, stirring constantly, until mixture thickens slightly. Pour over chicken and serve.

YIELD: 4 servings

CALORIES: 150
FAT GRAMS: 3
CALCIUM: 18 mg.
SODIUM: 95 mg.

FIBER: 1 gram
CHOLESTEROL: 71 mg.
IRON: 1 mg.

BARBECUED CHICKEN

12 oz. chicken breasts, skinless
Sauce:
1/2 tablespoon Worcestershire
    sauce
1 tablespoon reduced-sodium
    soy sauce

1/4 cup low-sugar catsup
1 tablespoon brown sugar
1 teaspoon lemon juice
1 garlic clove
1/4 teaspoon ground ginger

Combine all sauce ingredients. Marinate chicken in refrigerator for 1 hour. Grill chicken, brushing several times with remaining marinade.

YIELD: 4 3-ounce servings

CALORIES: 170

FIBER: 0

FAT GRAMS: 4

CHOLESTEROL: 49 mg.

CALCIUM: 18 mg.

IRON: 1 mg.

SODIUM: 373 mg.

CHICKEN PARMESAN

½ pound skinless and boneless chicken breasts
1 teaspoon dried basil
½ teaspoon dried oregano
½ teaspoon dried thyme
Pinch black pepper
3 egg whites

½ cup whole-wheat bread crumbs
2 ounces grated mozzarella cheese, low fat
1 tablespoon grated Parmesan cheese
8 ounces Ragú or Red Sauce (recipe page 148)

Preheat oven to 500 degrees. Apportion chicken into two 4-ounce pieces. Combine bread crumbs, basil, oregano, thyme and black pepper in a mixing bowl. Dip each piece of chicken in egg whites, then crumbs, pressing crumbs firmly into the meat. Arrange the chicken in a foil-lined baking pan. Bake for 15 minutes, or until done. Sprinkle the chicken with mozzarella and Parmesan, and return to the oven long enough to brown cheese. Serve with sauce.

Add pasta and salad to complete the meal.

YIELD: 2 4-ounce servings

CALORIES: 325

SODIUM: 360 mg.

FAT GRAMS: 8

FIBER: .5 grams

CALCIUM: 310 mg.

CHOLESTEROL: 85 mg.

SALMON WITH YOGURT DILL SAUCE

20 ounces raw Atlantic salmon
3 tablespoons prepared yellow
    mustard
1/2 cup nonfat yogurt
1 tablespoon olive oil
1/4 cup green onion (scallions),
    chopped

1 tablespoon white wine
    vinegar
1 tablespoon fresh dill, chopped
1/2 teaspoon fresh ground
    pepper
1 large lemon
8 sprigs fresh dill

Turn on broiler. Slice salmon into 4 equal 5-ounce portions. Whisk together mustard, yogurt, oil, green onion, vinegar, dill, and pepper. Rub juice of lemon on each piece of salmon. Then place two sprigs of fresh dill under the salmon and broil for 5 minutes or until fish flakes easily with a fork. Slowly heat yogurt sauce until warm. Pour on fish.

YIELD: 4 servings

CALORIES: 260
FAT GRAMS: 12
CALCIUM: 95 mg.
SODIUM: 232 mg.

FIBER: .3 grams
CHOLESTEROL: 79 mg.
IRON: 1.5 mg.

FRESH FISH FILLET WITH VEGGIES

2 fillets (5 ounces each) of fish
    (flat fish like flounder,
    sole, or yellowtail)
1/8 teaspoon pepper
1/2 cup orange juice
1/2 cup dry white wine
1 tablespoon orange liqueur

4 ounces baby carrots
12 asparagus spears
1 regular carrot, cut into
    julienne (very thin) strips
4 ounces leeks, cleaned and cut
    into julienne strips
1 teaspoon butter

Clean fish. Sprinkle with pepper. Pour orange juice and wine into skillet or nonstick frying pan. Add fillets and poach over medium heat for 8 minutes or until fish is cooked thoroughly. Drain liquid into saucepan and add liqueur. Cook to reduce the liquid (this concentrates the flavor). Steam baby carrots and asparagus in separate containers. Sauté julienned regular carrot with leeks in butter in nonstick pan until tender. Place baby carrots and asparagus on either side of fish and julienne mixture on top of fillet. Serve.

YIELD: 2 servings

CALORIES: 220
FAT GRAMS: 2.5
CALCIUM: 95 mg.
SODIUM: 83 mg.

FIBER: 4.2 grams
CHOLESTEROL: 5 mg.
IRON: 3 mg.

BAKED SNAPPER
WITH MUSTARD

1 pound red snapper
Marinade:
1/4 cup dry white wine
2 tablespoons chopped scallions
2 tablespoons Dijon mustard

1 1/2 tablespoons low-sodium soy
1 tablespoon honey
1 garlic clove, chopped
1 teaspoon curry powder
1/2 teaspoon cumin

Clean fish and pat dry. Spray vegetable oil into baking dish. Combine marinade and stir. Put fish in pan then add marinade for 30 minutes. Remove from marinade and broil or grill for 5 minutes on each side until fish flakes; baste during cooking.

YIELD: 4 servings

CALORIES: 220
FIBER: 0
CALCIUM: 45 mg.

FAT GRAMS: 3
CHOLESTEROL: 42 mg.
SODIUM: 200 mg.

HONEY SPICED FISH

1/2 pound raw red snapper or
flounder
1/3 cup room-temperature
water
1 beef bouillon cube, low
sodium
1 ounce dry sherry
Pinch aniseed

1/2 teaspoon lemon peel,
shredded
1 tablespoon chopped scallions
1 1/2 tablespoons red wine
vinegar
Pinch cumin
1/2 teaspoon mustard powder
1 tablespoon honey

Preheat oven to 325 degrees. Place fish in a casserole
dish. Add water, bouillon, sherry, aniseed, and lemon
peel. Let marinate in refrigerator for 1/2 hour. Then add
scallions, vinegar, cumin, mustard powder, and honey.
Let sit for 15 more minutes in refrigerator. Cover and
bake for 20 minutes or until fish flakes.

YIELD: 2 servings

CALORIES: Red snapper
175, flounder 180
FAT GRAMS: Red snapper
2.5, flounder 2
CALCIUM: 77 mg.

SODIUM: 172 mg.
CHOLESTEROL: 84 mg.
IRON: .7 mg.
FIBER: 0

CRAB CAKES

7 ounces canned low sodium
crab meat, rinsed well, or
fresh cooked crab
3 Kavli, Melba or other large
whole-grain crackers,
finely crushed
2 tablespoons minced onion
1/4 cup finely diced red pepper
2 tablespoons chopped parsley
2 egg whites, beaten

2 teaspoons reduced-calorie
mayonnaise
1 tablespoon lemon juice
1 teaspoon Worcestershire sauce
1/8 teaspoon ground red pepper
1 teaspoon basil
1/2 teaspoon marjoram
1 clove garlic, minced
Vegetable spray

Preheat oven to 375 degrees. Spray cookie sheet with vegetable spray. Mix all ingredients. Shape into 4 evenly sized patties. Heat for 20 minutes. Makes 4 cakes.

YIELD: 2 servings of 2 cakes each

CALORIES: 320

FAT GRAMS: 4

CALCIUM: 150 mg.

SODIUM: 213 mg.

FIBER: 2.3 grams

CHOLESTEROL: 90 mg.

IRON: 2.5 mg.

STIR-FRY TERIYAKI BEEF AND VEGETABLES

12 ounces steak (beef loin), trimmed and lean

2 tablespoons honey

1 tablespoon low-sodium soy sauce

2 ounces low-sodium chicken or beef stock

1 teaspoon fresh ginger or ½ teaspoon dried

4 cloves garlic, chopped

1 large green pepper, cut in strips

1 medium onion, chopped

2 cups chopped broccoli

4 ounces water chestnuts

1 cup sliced mushrooms

1 tomato, chopped

1 teaspoon sesame oil

Vegetable spray

Cut beef into strips. Whisk honey, soy, stock, ginger and garlic together; pour over beef and marinate for an hour in refrigerator. Spray wok with vegetable spray, add oil. Stir-fry steak, pepper, onion, broccoli, and water chestnuts. Cook briefly, then add mushrooms and tomatoes. Toss lightly and fry for a few more minutes.

YIELD: 4 servings

CALORIES: 280

FAT GRAMS: 8.5

CALCIUM: 51 mg.

SODIUM: 213 mg.

FIBER: 1.7 grams

CHOLESTEROL: 78 mg.

IRON: 4 mg.

BASIL & TOMATO QUICHE

*2 large tomatoes, peeled,
   seeded, diced*
8 basil leaves, chopped
3 egg whites
1 whole egg
1 cup evaporated skim milk
*1 1/2 cups grated part-skim
   mozzarella cheese*

2 tablespoons scallions
1/2 garlic clove, minced
Pinch white pepper
Pinch nutmeg
*2 tablespoons grated Parmesan
   cheese*
Vegetable spray

Preheat oven to 350 degrees. Spray an 8-by-8-inch glass baking dish with vegetable spray. In a mixing bowl, beat eggs, stir in milk, and add remaining ingredients, mixing well. Turn into the baking dish and bake for about 30 minutes. The quiche is done when a knife blade inserted into the center of it comes out clean.

YIELD: 8 servings

CALORIES: 115
FAT GRAMS: 4.5
CALCIUM: 260 mg.
SODIUM: 190 mg.

FIBER: 0.5 grams
CHOLESTEROL: 44 mg.
IRON: .7 mg.

Pastas and Rice

SPAGHETTI WITH WHITE-CLAM AND SHRIMP SAUCE

6 ounces linguini, dry

1 16-oz. can whole clams with juice (1 cup clams; 1 cup juice)

9 ounces cooked shrimp

1 tablespoon olive oil

4 cloves garlic, chopped (1 ½ tsp.)

1 pound (2 cups) whole tomatoes, chopped

¼ teaspoon red pepper flakes

½ teaspoon fresh ground black pepper

4 tablespoons fresh grated Parmesan cheese

½ cup chopped parsley

½ cup chopped fresh basil

Cook pasta for about 8 minutes. While pasta is cooking, open and drain clams, reserving liquid. Chop clams. Heat oil and garlic in a large pan. Sauté, then add tomatoes, clam juice, pepper flakes, black pepper, and bring to boil. Add partially cooked linguini and cook until al dente (about 4 or 5 more minutes). Add shrimp and clams. Toss in Parmesan cheese, parsley, and basil. Serve.

YIELD: 4 servings

CALORIES: 365

FAT GRAMS: 7

CALCIUM: 192 mg.

SODIUM: 765 mg.

FIBER: 2.5 grams

CHOLESTEROL: 47 mg.

IRON: 4.5 mg.

CHICKEN PASTA WITH PEPPER AND SUN-DRIED TOMATOES

3 ounces dry whole-wheat pasta

4 ounces chicken breast, raw

6 ounces roasted red peppers, sliced

3 ounces sun-dried tomatoes, cut in half (dry packed, no added oil or salt)

2 cloves garlic, chopped

1/4 cup green onion (scallions), chopped

1/4 cup Greek black olives, pits removed

Pinch black pepper

12 ounces chicken broth, low sodium

3/4 cup Red Sauce (recipe on page 148)

ROASTING A PEPPER:

There are two ways to roast a pepper. If you have a gas stove, turn the flame on high, and place the pepper directly into the flame until the skin is blistered and blackened, turning it occasionally. If you do not have a gas stove, place the peppers in a baking pan directly under the broiler in your oven, turning occasionally.

Cover the peppers with a towel and allow to cool. Rub the cooled peppers with your fingers or, using a paring knife, remove the blackened skin, peeling from top to bottom. Do not run the peppers under water to rinse them. This removes the roasted flavor. Remove the stems and seeds before using, and slice lengthwise into 1/4-inch strips.

Place pasta in boiling water to cook. While pasta is cooking, sauté chicken, peppers, rinsed tomato, garlic, green onion, black olives, and black pepper in a nonstick skillet over a high flame. Add the stock a little at a time, and bring to a high boil. Add cooked pasta and Red Sauce to skillet. Toss and serve.

YIELD: 2 1½-ounce servings

CALORIES: 300	FIBER: 3.5 grams
FAT GRAMS: 4.5	CHOLESTEROL: 33 mg.
CALCIUM: 58 mg.	IRON: 4 mg.
SODIUM: 200 mg.	

Modified from a recipe created by Michael McVay, formerly of the Doral Saturnia International Spa Resort.

EASY-TO-MAKE SPINACH-MUSHROOM LASAGNA

Combine the following ingredients and refrigerate the night before:

2 boxes frozen chopped spinach, steamed and drained
1 pint part-skim ricotta cheese
4 ounces grated part-skim mozzarella cheese

8 ounces 1% cottage cheese
3/4 cup grated Parmesan cheese
2 tablespoons dried Italian spice blend
3 cloves garlic, chopped
1 teaspoon ground pepper

Red Sauce:
Combine all of the following and cook at simmer for one hour.

30-ounce jar Ragú Homestyle spaghetti sauce
4 ounces tomato paste
1 16-ounce can low-sodium whole tomatoes
1/2 cup fresh basil leaves

3 cloves garlic, chopped
1 tablespoon dried Italian spice blend
1 cup sliced mushrooms
2 dashes Tabasco

Other items for lasagna:

12 whole-wheat, dry lasagna noodles (3/4 box)
1 cup water
4 more ounces part-skim

mozzarella
3 more cups fresh mushrooms
1 large red pepper, diced
Pam olive oil spray

Preheat oven to 350. Spray a 12-by-9-by-3-inch lasagna pan with Pam olive oil spray. Cover bottom of pan with red sauce. Layer 4 dry lasagna noodles, ½ of cheese-spinach mixture, 1 cup of mushrooms, another layer of 4 lasagna noodles, red sauce from recipe, the rest of cheese-spinach mixture, the last 2 cups of sliced mushrooms, and a final layer of 4 noodles. Cover with the rest of red sauce, 4 ounces of part-skim mozzarella, and chopped red pepper.

Pour 1 cup of water around the sides of the lasagna. Seal with aluminum foil and bake for 1½ hours. Poke with a fork to test for doneness. Let cool. Tastes better if made the previous day, then reheated.

YIELD: 12 servings

CALORIES: 330
FAT GRAMS: 10
CALCIUM: 435 mg.!!!
IRON: 4 mg.

FIBER: 3.6 gm
CHOLESTEROL: 28 mg.
SODIUM: 557 mg.

CARIBBEAN RICE

1 cup raw long-grain brown
   rice
½ cup low-sodium chicken
   broth
1 tablespoon sesame oil
2 ounces baby corn
4 ounces straw mushrooms or
   another kind of mushroom
2 ounces water chestnuts
1 carrot, chopped
1 tablespoon fresh chopped
   parsley

1 small onion, chopped
1 red pepper, chopped
1 green pepper, chopped
1 tablespoon low-sodium soy
   sauce
4 ounces cooked chicken breast,
   cut into bite-sized pieces
3 ounces frozen green peas
Vegetable spray

Cook rice according to instructions on package. Drain. In nonstick pan, spray vegetable spray, add chicken broth and sesame oil, then simmer corn, mushrooms, water chestnuts, carrots, parsley, onion, and peppers until tender. Mix soy, chicken, and rice in large, deep casserole dish. Blend in vegetables. Mix well. Preheat oven to 350 degrees. Bake casserole for 25 minutes. Cook peas as directed on package and add to casserole. Serve.

YIELD: 8 1¼-cup servings (or 6 1½-cup servings)

CALORIES: 290 (385)
FAT GRAMS: 5 (6.5)
CALCIUM: 40 mg.
IRON: 2 mg.

FIBER: 3 grams
CHOLESTEROL: 17 mg.
SODIUM: 118 mg.

Salads

HOT SPINACH SALAD

1 tablespoon olive oil
2 ounces red onion, sliced thin
1 tablespoon chopped garlic
6 ounces sliced mushrooms
⅓ cup balsamic vinegar

4 ounces roasted red peppers,
    peeled, cut in strips
4 ounces snow peas, sliced into
    thirds
1 pound raw spinach, cleaned

Cook onions and garlic in oil over high heat in a sauté pan. Add mushrooms. Then add balsamic vinegar and simmer until mushrooms and onions are limp. Add roasted peppers and snow peas and sauté over high heat for 1 minute. Remove from heat and toss with spinach. Best if served on warm plates.

YIELD: 2 salads

CALORIES: 185
FAT GRAMS: 7
CALCIUM: 226 mg.
IRON: 9.5 mg.

FIBER: 12 grams
SODIUM: 190 mg.
CHOLESTEROL: 0

Modified from a recipe created by Michael McVay, formerly of the Doral Saturnia International Spa Resort.

SHRIMP SALAD

8 ounces small frozen and thawed or canned cooked shrimp (low-sodium or rinsed canned shrimp)
1 hard-boiled egg, chopped fine
2 hard-boiled egg whites, chopped fine
1 cup celery, diced fine
1 medium onion, diced fine
2 tablespoons green onions, chopped fine
1 medium cucumber, peeled, seeded and diced
1 teaspoon lemon juice

Combine all shrimp salad ingredients, plus 4 tablespoons of Dill Dressing (p. 160) or low-fat commercial dill dressing in a bowl and chill. In ½ pita pocket, place ½ cup shrimp salad and Romaine lettuce; 2 slices of tomato and a pinch of bean sprouts may also be added for taste.

YIELD: 2 cups

SERVING SIZE: 4 ½-cup servings
CALORIES: 115
FAT GRAMS: 2
CALCIUM: 74 mg.
FIBER: 1 gram
CHOLESTEROL: 157 mg. with egg yolk, 98 mg. without egg yolk
SODIUM: 163 mg.

Modified recipe of the Doral Saturnia International Spa Resort.

CHICKEN SALAD

3 ounces cooked chicken breast,
   cut into bite-sized pieces
1 stalk celery, chopped
½ apple, diced finely
1 tablespoon raisins

1 tablespoon nonfat yogurt
1 tablespoon light mayonnaise
Pinch pepper
Pinch thyme
Pinch nutmeg

Mix all ingredients in bowl. Serve on various lettuces with 4 nonfat crackers such as Kavli or Ry-Krisp.

YIELD: 1 serving

CALORIES: 270
FAT GRAMS: 8
CALCIUM: 67 mg.
IRON: 1.3 mg.

FIBER: 2.7 grams
CHOLESTEROL: 78 mg.
SODIUM: 198 mg.

TURKEY, PASTA AND VEGETABLE SALAD

Place the following ingredients in a large bowl:

*8 ounces white turkey meat,
   roasted without skin*
*8 ounces cooked small pasta
   shells*
2 cups chopped tomato
1 zucchini, chopped

1 red pepper, chopped
1/2 cup celery
1/4 cup red onion
*4 ounces blanched, chilled
   Chinese pea pods*
4 ounces sliced mushrooms

Toss together the following ingredients and add to pasta mixture above:

1 tablespoon olive oil
2 teaspoons Dijon mustard
1 ounce red wine vinegar
1/2 cup lemon juice
2 tablespoons chopped scallions
4 garlic cloves, chopped
1/4 cup chopped basil

4 tablespoons chopped parsley
*2 tablespoons grated Parmesan
   cheese*
2 teaspoons dill weed
*1/2 teaspoon freshly ground
   pepper*

Chill 1 hour before serving.

YIELD: 6 2-cup servings

CALORIES: 285
FAT GRAMS: 7
CALCIUM: 106 mg.

FIBER: 3 grams
CHOLESTEROL: 30 mg.
SODIUM: 96 mg.

Veggies

SZECHUAN STRING BEANS

1 teaspoon sesame oil
2 cups fresh green beans,
   trimmed
2 tablespoons low sodium soy
   sauce
1 red pepper, finely diced
4 ounces canned water
   chestnuts, rinsed well,
   diced

2 garlic cloves, minced
1 tablespoon Szechuan
   flavoring
½ teaspoon black pepper
(black pepper to taste)
2 ounces chicken broth
Vegetable spray

Spray vegetable oil in a wok or nonstick frying pan. Add sesame oil at medium-high heat, then green beans. Toss for 7 minutes. Add all remaining ingredients. Toss and cook for an additional 5 minutes.

YIELD: 4 servings

CALORIES: 57
FAT GRAMS: 1.4
CALCIUM: 26 mg.
IRON: .5 mg.

FIBER: 1.6 grams
CHOLESTEROL: 0
SODIUM: 240 mg.

STUFFED ONIONS

4 large onions
4 ounces Canadian bacon (or
  diced low-salt ham),
  rinsed well, finely chopped
1/4 cup chopped parsley
1/2 cup bread crumbs, salt free

1 teaspoon marjoram
1 medium egg, beaten
2 tablespoons grated Parmesan
  cheese
1 small ripe tomato, chopped
Black pepper to taste

Preheat oven to 375 degrees. Hollow out onions, leaving shell 1/2 inch thick. Chop rest. Put in saucepan and cover with water. Cook about 5 minutes. Then, in a frying pan, over medium heat cook Canadian bacon until crisp and add remainder of chopped onion pieces. Cook until onions are translucent. Combine parsley, bread crumbs, marjoram in bowl. Add and mix breadcrumb mixture with bacon and onions. Add beaten egg, parmesan cheese, and pepper. Stir in tomato, then stuff in onion shells. Place stuffed onions on vegetable-sprayed baking dish. Cover with aluminum foil and bake for 1 hour. Cool for 5 minutes and serve.

YIELD: 4 servings

CALORIES: 210
FAT GRAMS: 5
CALCIUM: 119 mg.
IRON: 2 mg.
FIBER: 2 grams

CHOLESTEROL: 78 mg.
SODIUM: 600 mg. (much
  less if you rinse
  Canadian bacon
  before frying)

STUFFED ZUCCHINI

2 medium zucchini squash
Stuffing:
1/2 cup chopped onion
1 garlic clove, minced
2 tablespoons chicken stock
8 ounces fresh or frozen
    chopped spinach
1 cup cooked brown rice
1/2 cup cottage cheese
2 ounces part-skim mozzarella
    cheese

4 large fresh mushrooms,
    sliced
2 egg whites, beaten
2 tablespoons chopped parsley
2 teaspoons dried oregano
1 teaspoon low sodium soy
    sauce
1/4 teaspoon nutmeg
1/8 teaspoon paprika

Preheat oven to 350 degrees. Cut zucchini lengthwise and hollow out the centers. Steam zucchini for one minute. Sauté the onion and garlic in the chicken stock until onions look clear. Steam spinach and drain completely. Combine the rest of the ingredients and stuff zucchini. Sprinkle with paprika. Bake in casserole dish in oven for 1/2 hour. Serve.

YIELD: 4 servings

CALORIES: 120
FAT GRAMS: 1
CALCIUM: 101 mg.
IRON: 2.7 mg.

FIBER: 3 grams
CHOLESTEROL: 0 mg.
SODIUM: 250 mg.

Modified recipe of the Doral Saturnia International Spa Resort.

SWEET-POTATO PUREE

4 sweet potatoes
4 tablespoons honey
6 ounces orange juice (or the
   juice of 2 oranges)

1 teaspoon grated orange peel
1/2 teaspoon cinnamon
1/2 teaspoon nutmeg
1/4 teaspoon cloves

Cut sweet potatoes into quarters and boil until tender (about 15 minutes). Drain and cool. Put all other ingredients in food processor or blender and puree until smooth.

YIELD: 8 1/2-cup servings

CALORIES: 140
FAT GRAMS: 0
CALCIUM: 34 mg.
IRON: .6 mg.

FIBER: 3 grams
CHOLESTEROL: 0 mg.
SODIUM: 11 mg.

Sauces and Spreads

PESTO SAUCE

2 cups fresh basil (or 2½
    cups, if no fresh mint or
    coriander)
¼ cup fresh coriander
¼ cup mint leaves
2 tablespoons pine nuts
4 cloves garlic

2 ounces grated Parmesan
    cheese
2 tablespoons grated Romano
    cheese
1 tablespoon olive oil
¼ cup water

Place all ingredients in food processor or blender. Process until the ingredients form a smooth paste. Makes 1½ cups paste. Add and toss with cooked pasta or chicken. If you need a thinner, add a little water.

YIELD: 12 1-ounce servings of paste

CALORIES: 50
FAT GRAMS: 3.5
CALCIUM: 96 mg.
IRON: 1 mg.

CHOLESTEROL: 4 mg.
SODIUM: 109 mg.
FIBER: 0

"POTATO" SPREAD

1 cup 1% cottage cheese
1/3 cup nonfat plain yogurt
1 tablespoon Dijon mustard

2 tablespoons chopped chives
1 teaspoon black pepper

Combine cottage cheese and yogurt in blender until smooth. Combine with remaining ingredients in bowl and stir with wooden spoon.

YIELD: 6 2-ounce portions

CALORIES: 40
FAT GRAMS: .5
CALCIUM: 47 mg.
IRON: 1 mg.

FIBER: 0 grams
CHOLESTEROL: 0
SODIUM: 52 mg.

Modified from a recipe created by Michael McVay, formerly of the Doral Saturnia International Spa Resort.

BEAN SPREAD

10-ounce can kidney beans,
    rinsed
1 small onion
3 tablespoons catsup

1 tablespoon tomato paste
1 garlic clove, chopped
1/8 teaspoon cayenne
Pinch pepper (to taste)

Place all ingredients in a blender. Puree until smooth. Use as filling for burritos, tacos, or as dip for tortilla chips.

YIELD: 12 1-ounce servings or 2-Tbsp. servings

CALORIES: 28
FAT GRAMS: 0
CALCIUM: 10 mg.
IRON: .4 mg.
FIBER: 2 grams

CHOLESTEROL: 0
SODIUM: 128 mg. (will
    be less if beans are
    rinsed)

DILL DRESSING

1/2 cup cottage cheese, 1% fat
2 tablespoons low-fat
  mayonnaise
2 tablespoons fresh dill
1 shallot

1/4 teaspoon white pepper
1 1/2 teaspoons Dijon mustard
1 tablespoon lemon juice
1 dash Tabasco sauce

Combine all ingredients and blend at high speed in a blender. This dressing is very thick, and can be thinned with skimmed milk if it is to be used on a salad. If it is used as a dip for shrimp or vegetables, omit the milk and leave it thick. Chill well before serving.

YIELD: 6 1-ounce servings

CALORIES: 40
FAT GRAMS: 2
CALCIUM: 21 mg.

FIBER: 0
CHOLESTEROL: 2 mg.
SODIUM: 53 mg.

APPLE BUTTER

2 Golden Delicious apples,
  cored, sliced, with skin left
  on
1/2 tablespoon lemon juice
1/2 cup water

2 tablespoons apple juice
  concentrate
1/2 teaspoon cinnamon
1/2 teaspoon nutmeg
1/8 teaspoon ground cloves

Combine apples, lemon juice, and water. Simmer for 30 minutes or until apples are soft. Cool, then put in blender until smooth. Put into saucepan and add apple juice concentrate and spices. Simmer for 1 hour or until thickened.

YIELD: 16 1-tablespoon servings

CALORIES: 14

FIBER: .5 grams

FAT GRAMS: 0

CHOLESTEROL: 0

CALCIUM: 2 mg.

SODIUM: 1 mg.

IRON: 0 mg.

STRAWBERRY TOPPING FOR ANGEL-FOOD CAKE OR LOW-FAT ICE CREAM

1 1/2 cups fresh strawberries, cleaned and mashed
2/3 cup sugar

2 egg whites
1/8 teaspoon salt

Combine strawberries with remaining items in bowl and beat to form peaks (10 minutes).

YIELD: 12 servings (a heaping 2 tablespoons each)

CALORIES: 51

IRON: 0

FAT GRAMS: 0

CHOLESTEROL: 0 mg.

CALCIUM: 3 mg.

SODIUM: 38 mg.

FIBER: .4 gm.

Desserts

ANGEL-FOOD CAKE

1 1/2 cups egg whites (14 egg
    whites)
1 1/2 teaspoons cream of tartar
1/4 teaspoon salt
1 cup sugar

1 1/4 teaspoons vanilla
1 cup sifted cake flour, mixed
    with additional 1/2 cup
    granulated sugar

Preheat oven to 325 degrees. Beat egg whites until frothy and triple in volume. Add cream of tartar and salt and continue to beat until stiff. Add sugar and vanilla and continue beating. Add sifted flour and sugar a small amount at a time and fold into mixture. With a spatula, transfer the mixture to ungreased angel-food cake pan. Bake for 60 minutes. Let cake cool completely. Then slide thin knife around sides and bottom of cake. Invert on dish. Serve with or without strawberry topping.

YIELD: 12 slices

CALORIES: 140
FAT GRAMS: 0
CALCIUM: 5 mg.
SODIUM: 123 mg.

IRON: 0
CHOLESTEROL: 0
FIBER: 0

PUMPKIN PIE

1 cup canned pumpkin
1/2 cup evaporated skimmed
    milk
2 teaspoons vanilla
1 teaspoon cinnamon
1/4 teaspoon nutmeg

Pinch ginger
1 envelope unflavored gelatin
1/2 cup boiling water
1/4 cup apple juice concentrate
3 egg whites

Combine pumpkin, evaporated milk, vanilla, cinnamon, nutmeg, and ginger. Stir gelatin into boiling water until dissolved, then add apple juice concentrate. Combine all ingredients, mix well and put in refrigerator for 20 minutes. Beat egg whites until peaks form and fold into refrigerated pie mixture. Put in pie pan and chill until firm.

YIELD: 4 ½-cup portions

CALORIES: 60
CALCIUM: 61 mg.
FIBER: .6 gm.
IRON: .7 mg.

CHOLESTEROL: 1 mg.
SODIUM: 54 mg.
FAT GRAMS: 0

PEARS IN CIDER
WITH GINGER

2 medium pears
2 cups apple cider

1 ounce crystallized ginger

Peel pears. Put in large saucepan and pour in cider. Cover and bring to a boil, then simmer without lid for 30 minutes until pears are tender and there is a little cider syrup left in saucepan. Add ginger and let cool. Put in refrigerator and serve chilled.

YIELD: 4 ½-pear portions

CALORIES: 131
FAT GRAMS: .5
CALCIUM: 34 mg.
FIBER: 2.3 grams

IRON: 2 mg.
CHOLESTEROL: 0
SODIUM: 8 mg.

CARROT RAISIN CAKE WITH SLICED STRAWBERRIES

³/₄ cup whole-wheat flour
³/₄ cup all-purpose flour
2 teaspoons baking powder
¹/₂ teaspoon baking soda
¹/₂ teaspoon salt
1 teaspoon cinnamon
¹/₂ teaspoon nutmeg

¹/₂ cup sugar
2 ounces raisins
1 medium egg
¹/₂ cup nonfat yogurt
2 tablespoons corn oil
1 cup grated carrots
2 cups sliced fresh strawberries

Preheat oven to 350 degrees. Combine flours, baking powder, baking soda, salt, and spices in bowl. Combine sugar, raisins, egg, yogurt, oil and carrots. Mix all ingredients. Vegetable-spray 9-by-11-inch baking pan and spread batter in pan. Bake for 20 minutes. Cut 5 rows horizontally and 3 columns vertically (3 inches by 2¼ inches). Top with strawberries. Serve.

YIELD: 15 servings

CALORIES: 115
FAT GRAMS: 2
CALCIUM: 0 mg.
FIBER: 2 grams

IRON: 0 mg.
CHOLESTEROL: 20 mg.
SODIUM: 160 mg.

Modified recipe of the Doral Saturnia International Spa Resort.

APPLE BLUEBERRY RAISIN CRISP

2 pounds (6 cups) apples,
   cored and sliced (leave
   skin on)
1 pint fresh or frozen
   blueberries
1 tablespoon lemon juice
1/2 cup apple or orange juice
3/4 cup raisins
2 cups Quaker Oats
1/2 cup whole-wheat flour

1/4 cup oat flour
3 tablespoons margarine or
   butter
1/2 cup brown sugar
1 1/2 teaspoons cinnamon
1/4 teaspoon nutmeg
1/4 teaspoon allspice
1/4 teaspoon ground cloves
Vegetable spray

Preheat oven to 350 degrees. Spray vegetable spray in a 9-by-11-inch Teflon baking pan. Mix apples, blueberries, lemon juice, apple or orange juice, and raisins in a bowl. Mix oats, flours, butter, brown sugar, cinnamon, nutmeg, allspice, and ground cloves in a separate bowl. Put apple mixture in pan and top with oat mixture. Bake for 25 minutes.

YIELD: 25 2-ounce servings

CALORIES: 100
FAT GRAMS: 2
CALCIUM: 3 mg.

FIBER: 2 grams
CHOLESTEROL: 4 mg.
SODIUM: 5 mg.

Modified from a recipe created by Michael McVay, formerly of the Doral Saturnia International Spa Resort.

NINE

THE DIET DATA BANK
*How to Read a Label, Substitute Right Foods
for Wrong and Count Fat Grams*

HOW TO READ A LABEL

The following hints for reading labels will help you to become more knowledgeable about the foods you are buying and eating.

1. Calories and nutrients on a label are listed per serving. Check the serving size and the number of servings per container.

2. Fat grams are listed on a label. (28 grams = 1 ounce.) One gram of fat equals 9 calories. Fat calories are *not* listed on a label.

To find the percentage of fat: multiply the fat grams by 9, then divide that number by the total calories. For example, a piece of American cheese has 9 grams of fat and 105 calories.

$9 \times 9 = 81; 81 \div 105 = 77\%$ fat!

3. Sodium content per serving is listed in milligrams (mg.). The adequate daily dietary intake of sodium is 1,100 to 3,300 mg. An easy way to estimate if the sodium is within the guidelines suggested by the American Dietetic Association is to allow 1 mg. of sodium per calorie. Try not to go over 2 mg. of sodium per calorie. 1 gram = 1,000 mg. (1 teaspoon = over 2,000 mg.)

4. Cholesterol is not always listed on a label. When it *is* included, it is listed per serving or per 100 grams. Current recommendations from the American Heart Association suggest that cholesterol be kept under 300 mg. per day.

5. The percentage of U.S. Recommended Daily Allowances (USRDA) is the recommended daily amount of nutrients considered adequate for meeting the known nutritional needs of healthy persons. These are listed as percentages of the RDAs supplied by one serving of the food product.

6. A list of ingredients may be all you will find on some packages. Unfortunately, unless a product makes a nutritional claim of added vitamins or minerals, the label doesn't have to display any nutritional information. The key to remember is that all ingredients are listed in the order of their amount in weight in the package.

TERMS TO KNOW

Percent Fat Free is the weight of fat in the food, not the fat calories. For example, the composition of 2 percent milk is such that 36 percent of its calories come from fat. A turkey hot dog that is "80% fat free" actually gets 70 percent of its calories from fat! Turkey breast that is labeled 97 percent fat free is actually 25 percent fat. Read the grams of fat!

Light or *Lite* can refer to color, flavor, weight or texture. These terms are not defined by government regulation, except for processed meats which have at least 25 percent less fat than usual. Light foods may still contain fat. Light olive oil is just a lighter color of oil.

Reduced calorie foods have at least a third fewer calories than the foods they imitate. Typically, the comparisons are right on the label.

Low-calorie foods have less than 40 calories per serving. *"No cholesterol"* or *"Cholesterol free"* does not indicate anything about the fat content in a food product. Vegetable oils naturally do not contain cholesterol because they are not of animal origin. However, 100 percent of their calories come from fat. Vegetable shortenings may be cholesterol free, but they are filled with saturated fat, which boosts the cholesterol level in the blood.

Unsalted or *No added salt* means that salt has not been added during the processing of the food. However, these foods may still be high in sodium from components such as soy. Look for products that are labeled *sodium free* or *very low sodium.*

Reduced sodium means that the usual sodium content has been reduced by at least 75 percent; *low sodium* products contain 140 mg. or less of sodium per serving, *very low sodium* products contain 35 mg. of sodium or less, *sodium free* products contain less than 5 mg. of sodium per serving.

Natural is a term that has no official definition except when referring to meat products. Then, "natural" indicates a claim that the food has been minimally processed and is free of artificial ingredients or coloring. A natural cereal may be loaded with saturated fat.

High in fiber or *Good source of fiber* are claims manufacturers loosely apply to foods with minimal fiber. Only those foods with at least 3 grams of fiber are considered to be good fiber sources.

Fortified indicates that the product contains components that were not present naturally. Cereals are fortified with vitamins and minerals. Enriched foods are products that have lost their nutrients during processing; some, but not all, of these nutrients have been replaced. White rice, white bread, and white pastas are examples of enriched foods.

FOOD SUBSTITUTIONS

Replacing the Bad with the Good

1. Substitute evaporated skim milk for half-and-half or heavy cream.
2. Substitute 1% cottage cheese for whole milk ricotta.
3. Substitute nonfat yogurt or "yogurt cheese" for cream cheese or mayonnaise in recipes. (Since yogurt separates when heated, add 1 tablespoon of cornstarch to it before cooking.) Yogurt-cheese recipes are available in a book that can be ordered from Millhopper Marketing (904) 373–5800.
4. Buy an immersion blender (a handheld aerating appliance) so you can whip up skim milk to take the place of heavy whipping cream for desserts. Chilled evaporated skim milk can also be whipped. Add vanilla, egg white and a little sugar for flavor.
5. Use two egg whites for each whole egg called for in a recipe. When making omelets or scrambled eggs, use all egg whites or one egg and two egg whites.
6. In recipes calling for 1 ounce of unsweetened chocolate, use 1/4 cup cocoa mixed with two tablespoons of oil, butter, margarine or shortening.
7. Halve the sugar in recipes and substitute molasses, very ripe bananas, pineapples, dried fruits or apples, oranges, pineapples, or grape juice to sweeten the taste.
8. Instead of eating ice cream, try sorbets, frozen low-fat or nonfat yogurt, fruit-juice bars, low-calorie frozen fruit bars, ice milk or "fake fat" ice cream.
9. Use whole-grain brown rice, whole-grain pasta, bread and cereals instead of their nutrient-depleted white counterparts.
10. Substitute ground, spiced turkey for beef in chili, meat loaf, meatballs, or hamburgers.

11. Substitute bouillon, herbs, wine or juices for high-fat sauces and gravies.
12. Use water chestnuts instead of nuts for that crunchy taste in recipes.
13. Eat unsalted pretzels instead of nuts, buttered popcorn or chips.
14. Try angel food cake (zero fat) instead of high-fat cakes.
15. Substitute all-fruit jam for high-sugar jam.
16. Try apple butter as a spread instead of real butter or margarine. It's fat-free and much lower in calories.

FAT-GRAM COUNTER

Nutritional information does *not* appear on every label of a packaged food. Nutritional labeling is *voluntary* unless a specific claim is made about the contents, such as "low sodium." Hence, it is very important to familiarize yourself with the contents of foods you eat. The following chart should help make you an informed consumer—and a better dieter.

PROTEINS

Food Item	Amount	Calories	Fat Grams
BEEF:			
Chuck, lean & fat, cooked	3½ oz.	330	24
Eye of Round	3½ oz.	175	6
Frankfurter	1 frank	180	16
Ground:			
Lean	3½ oz.	270	19
Regular	4 oz.	324	23
Rib Roast	4 oz.	273	15
Salami, cooked	3½ oz.	260	21
Steak:			
Flank, lean	3½ oz.	245	15
Porterhouse, lean	3½ oz.	220	11
Sirloin, lean	3½ oz.	210	9
LAMB:			
Chop, broiled	3½ oz.	190	8
Leg, lean, roasted	3½ oz.	185	7
PORK:			
Bacon:			
Canadian	2 slices	90	4
Crisp	2 slices	75	6
Frankfurter			
Pork & beef	1 frank	145	13
Ham:			
Packaged, lean	1 slice	35	1.5
Cured, roasted	3½ oz.	180	9
Pork Chop	4 oz.	392	31
Sausage, cooked	4 oz.	455	43
Spareribs, cooked	3½ oz.	395	30
POULTRY:			
Chicken:			
Breast w/ skin	3½ oz.	195	8

Food Item	Amount	Calories	Fat Grams
Breast w/o skin, roasted	3½ oz.	165	4
Wing w/ skin	3½ oz.	290	20
Duck, w/ skin, roasted	3½ oz.	335	28
Egg	1 med.	70	5
Egg White	1 ea.	15	0
Frankfurter, turkey	1 frank	100	8
Turkey:			
Dark meat, w/o skin	4 oz.	210	8
White meat, w/o skin	4 oz.	180	4

VEAL:

Cutlet, breaded	4 oz.	245	9
Lean, roasted	3½ oz.	185	6

VEGETARIAN PROTEINS:

Chick-peas, cooked	½ cup	135	2
Lentils, cooked	½ cup	115	0
Split Peas, cooked	½ cup	115	1
Tofu, firm	4 oz.	95	5

FISH:

Fin Fish, Uncooked:

Bass	4½ oz.	125	3
Flounder	4½ oz.	85	1
Salmon:			
Canned	4 oz.	160	8
Fresh	4½ oz.	190	8
Snapper, Red	4½ oz.	125	2
Sole	4½ oz.	90	1
Trout, Rainbow	4½ oz.	150	4
Tuna:			
In Oil, drained	4 oz.	225	9
In Water, drained	4 oz.	140	2

Shellfish:

Clams, Atlantic	4½ oz.	105	1

Food Item	Amount	Calories	Fat Grams
Crab:			
Blue, cooked	4½ oz.	130	1
Canned	4 oz.	115	3
Lobster	4 oz.	110	2
Mussels	4½ oz.	110	3
Oysters	4½ oz.	80	3
Scallops	3 oz. (6 lg., 14 sm.)	75	.6
Shrimp:			
Canned	4 oz.	130	1
Fresh	4 oz.	110	2
CHEESE:			
American	1 oz.	105	9
Blue	1 oz.	100	8
Brie	1 oz.	95	8
Camembert	1 oz.	85	7
Cheddar	1 oz.	115	9
Cottage Cheese, creamed	½ cup	115	5
Dry Curd	½ cup	95	0
1% fat	½ cup	81	1
2% fat	½ cup	102	2
Cream Cheese	1 oz.	100	10
Light Philadelphia Brand (Kraft)	1 oz.	60	5
Reduced (Weight Watchers)	1 oz.	30	1
Whipped	1 oz.	85	8
Edam	1 oz.	105	8
Farmer	1 oz.	100	7
Feta:			
Natural, cow's milk	1 oz.	75	6
Flavored Spreads (Kraft):			
Jalapeño	1 oz.	65	5
Olive & Pimento	1 oz.	65	5
Goat	1 oz.	75	6

Food Item	Amount	Calories	Fat Grams
Gouda	1 oz.	100	8
Gruyère	1 oz.	115	9
Monterey Jack	1 oz.	95	8
Mozzarella, part skim	1 oz.	70	5
Parmesan:			
Grated	1 Tbsp	20	2
Hard	1 oz.	110	7
Pasteurized Process:			
(Kraft) Free	1 oz.	45	0
Light 'n Lively (Kraft)	1 oz.	70	4
Lite-Line (Borden's)	1 oz.	50	2
Ricotta	¼ cup	110	8
Ricotta, part skim	¼ cup	85	5
Romano	1 oz.	110	8
Roquefort	1 oz.	105	9
Swiss	1 oz.	105	8

CREAM:

Food Item	Amount	Calories	Fat Grams
Half-and-Half	2 Tbsp.	40	3
Heavy	2 Tbsp.	105	11
Sour cream	2 Tbsp.	50	5
Ice Cream:			
(Ben & Jerry's)	½ cup	295	18
(Breyers)	½ cup	155	9
(Carvel)	½ cup	110	2
Dove Bar	6 oz.	500	38
(Häagen-Dazs), vanilla	½ cup	250	17
(Sealtest)	½ cup	145	7
(Weight Watchers)	½ cup	90	1

MILK:

Food Item	Amount	Calories	Fat Grams
Ice Milk:			
(Breyers Light)	½ cup	130	4
(Frusen Glädjé)	½ cup	260	17
(Light 'n Lively)	½ cup	115	3
(Sealtest Free)	½ cup	100	0
(Weight Watchers)	½ cup	115	3
Milk:			
Buttermilk	8 oz.	100	2

Food Item	Amount	Calories	Fat Grams
Chocolate, 2%	8 oz.	180	5
Condensed	4 oz.	490	13
Evaporated, skim	4 oz.	100	0
Evaporated, whole	4 oz.	170	10
Low-fat 1%	8 oz.	100	3
Low-fat 2%	8 oz.	120	5
Skim	8 oz.	90	0
Whole 4%	8 oz.	160	9
Products Made with Milk:			
Carnation Instant			
Breakfast	1 serving	130	1
Pudding w/ whole milk	½ cup	195	6
Sherbet	1 cup	280	1
Yogurt:			
Low-fat, fruit	1 cup	225	2.5
Low-fat, plain	1 cup	140	3.5
Nonfat, plain	1 cup	110	0
Plain	1 cup	140	7
Yogurt, frozen:			
(Colombo)	¾ cup	150	3
(Dannon)	¾ cup	160	3
(Skinny Dip)	¾ cup	55	0
(TCBY)	¾ cup	190	0
(Tuscan)	¾ cup	360	19
(Yoplait)	¾ cup	180	4

FRUITS & VEGETABLES

FRUITS & FRUIT JUICES:

Apple	1 med.	80	0
Apple Juice	½ cup	60	0
Applesauce, unsweetened	½ cup	55	0
Apricot:			
Canned, heavy syrup	½ cup	105	0
Dried	½ cup	155	0
Fresh, whole	1 med.	15	0
Banana	1 med.	110	0
Blackberries	½ cup	40	0

Food Item	Amount	Calories	Fat Grams
Blueberries	½ cup	40	0
Cantaloupe	1 cup	60	0
Cherries	10 ea.	50	0
Cranberries	½ cup	25	0
Cranberry Juice Cocktail	½ cup	75	0
Cranberry Sauce, canned	½ cup	200	0
Dates, dried, pitted	½ cup	245	0
Fig, raw	1	50	0
Grapefruit	½ ea.	40	0
Grapefruit Juice	½ cup	50	0
Grape Juice	½ cup	75	0
Grapes	½ cup	60	0
Honeydew, raw	¼ sm.	35	0
Kiwifruit	1 med.	45	0
Lemon	1 med.	15	0
Lemonade, frozen	1 cup	105	0
Lime	1 med.	20	0
Mango	1 cup	105	0
Nectarine	1 med.	65	0
Orange	1 med.	60	0
Orange Juice	½ cup	55	0
Papaya	1 med.	115	0
Peaches:			
Canned/heavy syrup	½ cup	95	0
Fresh	1 med.	40	0
Pears:			
Canned/heavy syrup	½ cup	95	0
Canned/own juice	½ cup	60	0
Fresh	1 med.	100	0
Pineapple:			
Canned/heavy syrup	½ cup	100	0
Canned/own juice	½ cup	75	0
Fresh	½ cup	40	0
Pineapple Juice	½ cup	65	0
Plums	2 ea.	70	0
Prune Juice	½ cup	90	0
Prunes:			
Dried	2 ea.	40	0

Food Item	Amount	Calories	Fat Grams
Raw	½ cup	195	0
Stewed, unsweetened	½ cup	115	0
Raisins, seedless	¼ cup	115	0
Raspberries	½ cup	30	0
Strawberries	½ cup	20	0
Tangerines	1 med.	40	0
Watermelon	1 cup	50	0
VEGETABLES:			
Alfalfa Sprouts	½ cup	10	0
Artichoke Hearts	½ cup	30	0
Asparagus, spears	6 ea.	20	0
Avocado, fresh	½ med.	160	15
Bamboo Shoots, raw	¼ cup	10	0
Bean, green or wax	½ cup	20	0
Bean Sprouts	½ cup	15	0
Beets, diced, cooked	½ cup	30	0
Broccoli	½ cup	10	0
Brussels Sprouts	6–8 med.	30	0
Cabbage	½ cup	5	0
Carrots	1 med.	30	0
Cauliflower	1 cup	25	0
Celery, diced	½ cup	10	0
Coleslaw	½ cup	59	5
Cucumber	½ cup	10	0
Eggplant, cooked, diced	½ cup	15	0
Lettuce:	½ cup	5	0
Iceberg	3½ oz.	15	0
Romaine	3½ oz.	20	0
Mushrooms, raw	10 sm.	30	0
Okra	½ cup	20	0
Onions, sliced	½ cup	25	0
Peppers, all types	½ cup	20	0
Pickles, dill	1 lg.	15	0
Pumpkin, canned	½ cup	40	0
Radishes	½ cup	10	0
Relish, sweet	2 Tbsp	40	0
Sauerkraut, bottled	½ cup	20	0

Food Item	Amount	Calories	Fat Grams
Soybeans	½ cup	130	6
Spinach	½ cup	40	0
Squash:			
Butternut, baked	½ cup	40	0
Spaghetti, cooked	½ cup	25	0
Summer, boiled	½ cup	20	0
Winter, baked	½ cup	40	0
Tomato:			
Juice	½ cup	20	0
Raw	1 ea.	25	0
Sauce	½ cup	35	0
Turnip, cooked	½ cup	15	0
Water Chestnuts:			
Canned	½ cup	35	0
Zucchini:			
Cooked	½ cup	15	0
Raw	½ cup	10	0

HIGH-CARBOHYDRATE VEGETABLES:

Food Item	Amount	Calories	Fat Grams
Beans:			
Black, cooked	½ cup	120	0
Garbanzo, cooked	½ cup	135	0
Kidney, cooked	½ cup	109	0
Pinto, cooked	½ cup	115	1
Refried, w/ fat	½ cup	210	9
Refried, w/o fat	½ cup	135	1
Corn	½ cup	90	1
Corn on the Cob	1 ea.	80	1
Lentils, cooked	½ cup	115	0
Peas:			
Blackeye, cooked	½ cup	110	1
Green, cooked	½ cup	65	0
Split, cooked	½ cup	115	0
Potato:			
Baked w/ skin	1 med.	110–147	0
Chip	1 oz.	149	10
French fried	20	222	9

Food Item	Amount	Calories	Fat Grams
Sweet Potato:			
Baked	1 ea.	115	0

BREADS, CEREALS & GRAINS

BREADS, CRACKERS AND NOODLES:

Bagels:			
Plain:			
(Lender's)	1 ea.	165	1
(Sara Lee)	1 ea.	235	1
Biscuits, baking powder	1 med.	90	3
Bread:			
Banana nut	1 slice	135	6
Corn Bread	1 piece	200	7
Cracked wheat	1 slice	65	0
French	1 slice	80	1
Pita pockets, 6″	1 ea.	80	0
Pita, whole-wheat	1 med.	120	1
Pumpernickel	1 slice	80	1
Raisin	1 slice	70	1
Rye	1 slice	65	1
Sourdough	1 slice	75	0
White	1 slice	70	1
Whole-wheat	1 slice	70	1
Bread crumbs	¼ cup	100	1
Breadsticks	2 ea.	80	1
Bun, hamburger/hot dog	1 ea.	115	2
Crackers:			
Akmak	2 ea.	45	1
Graham	4 sqs.	120	3
Kavli	2 ea.	30	0
Matzo	1 ea.	115	0
Melba Toast	5 rounds	60	2
Ritz (Nabisco)	6 ea.	105	6
Ry Krisps (Ralston)	1 whole	25	0
Saltine	6 ea.	80	2
Sesame	6 ea.	105	3
Triscuit (Nabisco)	2 ea.	40	2
Wheat Thins	4 ea.	35	2

Food Item	Amount	Calories	Fat Grams
Croissants, frozen	1 med.	110	6
English muffins	1 ea.	135	1
Lasagna Noodles, cooked	1½ oz.	160	0
Macaroni, cooked	1 cup	160	1
Muffins:			
Blueberry	1 med.	150	7
Bran	1 med.	112	5
Rice Cakes	2 ea.	70	0
Rolls:			
Cinnamon	1 med.	220	8
Dinner	1 med.	110	2
Hard, white	1 med.	155	2
Whole-wheat	1 med.	90	1
Spaghetti, cooked	1 cup	160	1
Tortilla:			
Chips	10 ea.	135	7
Corn	1–6" ea.	65	1
Flour	1 med.	95	2
Waffle, frozen, round	1 med.	95	3

CEREALS:

Food Item	Amount	Calories	Fat Grams
40% bran flakes	½ cup	125	1
100% Natural (Quaker)	1 oz. (¼ cup)	135	6
All Bran (Kellogg's)	1 oz. (⅓ cup)	70	.5
Bran			
Oat	¼ cup	85	2
Wheat	¼ cup	40	0
Bran-Buds (Kellogg's)	1 oz. (⅓ cup)	70	1
Bran Chex (Ralston)	1 oz. (⅔ cup)	90	1
Cheerios (General Mills)	1 cup	110	2
Common Sense Oat Bran (Kellogg's)	⅔ cup	100	0
Corn Flakes	1 cup	100	0

Food Item	Amount	Calories	Fat Grams
Cream of Rice	1 cup	130	0
Cream of Wheat	1 cup	135	1
Crunchy Bran High (Quaker)	1 oz.	90	1
Fiber One (General Mills)	1 oz. (½ cup)	60	1
Granola with Raisins	1 cup	520	20
Grape-Nuts (Post)	1 oz. (¼ cup)	105	0
Just Right (Kellogg's)	1 oz. (¾ cup)	100	0
Nutri-Grain (Kellogg's)			
Corn	1 oz. (⅔ cup)	110	1
Wheat	1 oz. (¾ cup)	100	0
Wheat and barley	1 oz. (¾ cup)	100	1
Oat Bran Flakes	1 oz.	110	2
Oatmeal	1 cup	145	2
Product 19 (Kellogg's)	1 cup	145	0
Puffed Rice (Quaker)	1 cup	60	0
Puffed Wheat (Quaker)	1 oz.	105	0
Raisin Bran			
Chex	1 oz. (⅔ cup)	90	1
(Kellogg's)	1.3 oz. (¾ cup)	115	.7
(Post)	1 oz. (½ cup)	85	.5
Rice Chex (Ralston)	1 cup	100	0
Rice Krispies (Kellogg's)	1 oz. (1 cup)	110	0
Shredded Wheat	1 biscuit	85	0
Shredded Wheat 'n Bran (Nabisco)	1 oz.	110	1
Special K (Kellogg's)	1 oz. (1⅓ cups)	110	0

Food Item	Amount	Calories	Fat Grams
Total (General Mills)	1 oz. (1 cup)	100	.6
Wheat Chex (Ralston)	1 oz. (1 cup)	150	.7
Wheaties (General Mills)	1 oz. (1 cup)	100	.5

GRAINS:

Barley	½ cup	390	1
Bulgur, cooked	½ cup	190	0
Rice:			
Brown, cooked	½ cup	110	0
White, cooked	½ cup	110	0
Wild, cooked	½ cup	85	1

MISCELLANEOUS

ALCOHOLIC BEVERAGES:

Beer			
Light	12 oz.	110	0
Regular	12 oz.	145	0
Champagne	4 oz.	85	0
Gin, Rum, Vodka, Whiskey	1 oz.	70	0
Sherry	2 oz.	85	0
Vermouth, dry, French	3½ oz.	105	0
Wine, table	4 oz.	95	0

NON-ALCOHOLIC BEVERAGES:

Coffee	6 oz.	4	0
Fruit Punch	8 oz.	107	0
Sodas:			
Diet	12 oz.	0	0
Coca-Cola	12 oz.	150	0
Cream Soda	12 oz.	190	0
Fruit Flavored	12 oz.	170	0
Ginger Ale	12 oz.	125	0
Root Beer	12 oz.	150	0
Sprite	12 oz.	140	0
Tea	6 oz.	2	0

Food Item	Amount	Calories	Fat Grams

DESSERTS & SWEETS:

Food Item	Amount	Calories	Fat Grams
Apple Strudel (Sara Lee)	1 piece	280	17
Brownies:			
Plain	1 ea.	220	12
With nuts	1 ea.	265	16
Cakes:			
Angel Food, plain	1 piece	160	0
Carrot	1 piece	250	11
Cheesecake	1 piece	300	14
Cheesecake (Sara Lee)	1 slice	230	11
Coffee	1 slice	341	11
Cupcake, plain, no icing	1 med.	91	4
Fat-Free Loaf			
(Entenmann's)	1 oz.	70	2
Pound, plain	1 piece	305	18
Sponge, plain	1 piece	190	3
Strawberry Shortcake	1 piece	345	9
White, yellow and chocolate:			
Plain	1 piece	195	7
With icing	1 piece	230	8
Candy:			
Almond Joy	2 oz.	260	14
Baby Ruth	1 ea.	255	11
Butterfinger	1 ea.	215	10
Caramels, plain	1 oz.	113	3
Chocolate:			
Milk, plain	1 oz.	147	9
Milk, w/ almonds	1 oz.	120	8
Milk, w/ peanuts	1 oz.	159	12
Semisweet	1 oz.	144	10
Gumdrops	1 oz.	98	0
Hard Candies	1 oz.	109	0
Jelly Beans	1 oz.	104	0
Licorice	1 oz.	99	0
M&M's			
Peanut	1.6 oz.	240	12
Plain	1.6 oz.	220	10

Food Item	Amount	Calories	Fat Grams
Milky Way	2 oz.	260	9
Reese's Peanut Butter			
Cups	2 ea.	245	14
Snickers	2 oz.	270	13
3 Musketeers	2.3 oz.	280	8
Cookies:			
Butter	1 ea.	23	1
Chocolate chip w/ nuts	2 ea.	140	9
Chocolate chip, 2″	1 ea.	52	3
Bordeaux (Pepperidge			
Farm)	2 ea.	80	4
Fig Newtons (Nabisco)	2 ea.	110	2
Fortune Cookie, Chinese			
restaurant	2 ea.	45	0
Ginger Snaps (Nabisco)	2 ea.	70	2
(Health Valley)	3 ea.	75	1
Oatmeal Raisin	2 ea.	125	5
Oreo (Nabisco)	6 ea.	310	13
Peanut Butter	2 ea.	205	12
Vanilla Wafers	3 ea.	50	2
Danish:			
Cheese	1 ea.	254	12
Fruit	1 ea.	230	13
Doughnut	1 ea.	155	6
Eclair	1 ea.	250	13
Fruit & Fitness Bar (Health			
Valley)	1 ea.	200	5
Fruit Bar (Health Valley)	1 ea.	140	1
Fruit Muffin (Health			
Valley)	1 ea.	130	1
Granola Bar w/ raisins	1 bar	130	5
Pies: ⅛ of 9″ pie = 1 slice			
Apple	1 slice	280	12
Banana Custard	1 slice	250	11
Cherry	1 slice	310	13
Chocolate, chiffon	1 slice	265	12
Coconut Cream, frozen	1 slice	260	16.5

Food Item	Amount	Calories	Fat Grams
Custard	1 slice	250	13
Lemon Meringue, ⅙ of pie	1 slice	350	13
Pecan	1 slice	430	23.5
Pumpkin	1 slice	250	13
Strawberry	1 slice	185	7
Pudding	½ cup	180	5
Mousse, chocolate	½ cup	170	8

CONDIMENTS & BASICS:

Food Item	Amount	Calories	Fat Grams
Apple Butter	1 Tbsp.	41	0
Butter	1 Tbsp.	100	11
Butter	1 pat	70	8
Butter	1 tsp.	35	4
Catsup:			
Lite (Heinz)	1 Tbsp.	8	0
Regular	1 Tbsp.	16	0
Honey	1 Tbsp.	65	0
Horseradish	1 Tbsp.	5	0
Jam or Preserves:			
Low-calorie	1 Tbsp.	32	0
Regular	1 Tbsp.	54	0
Jelly	1 Tbsp.	55	0
Maple Syrup:			
Lite	1 oz.	60	0
Regular	1 oz.	100	0
Margarine	1 tsp.	35	4
Diet	1 tsp.	15	2
Regular	1 Tbsp.	101	11
Mayonnaise:			
Low-calorie	1 Tbsp.	21	2
Miracle Whip	1 Tbsp.	70	7
Regular	1 Tbsp.	99	11
Mustard:			
Brown	1 Tbsp.	15	0
Yellow	1 Tbsp.	12	0
Oil	1 tsp.	35	4

Food Item	Amount	Calories	Fat Grams
Olives:			
Black	10	60	7
Green	10	45	5
Peanut Butter	1 Tbsp.	95	8
Pickles:			
Dill	1 ea.	5	0
Sweet	1 ea.	50	0
Sugar, white/brown	1 Tbsp.	49	0
Vegetable Cooking Spray	½ oz.	28	0
Vegetable Shortening	1 Tbsp.	113	13
Vinegar, cider	1 Tbsp.	2	0

SELECTED DRESSINGS:

Italian/Vinaigrette/Oil-&-Vinegar Dressings:

Food Item	Amount	Calories	Fat Grams
Creamy Italian:			
(Kraft)	1 Tbsp.	60	5
(Wish-Bone)	1 Tbsp.	60	5
Italian Style:			
Low-calorie	1 Tbsp.	18	2
Regular	i Tbsp.	69	7
Olive Oil and Vinegar			
(Newman's Own)	1 Tbsp.	80	8
Savory Herb (Hain)	1 Tbsp.	90	10
Vinegar & Oil	1 Tbsp.	72	8

Light/Vinaigrette/Oil Dressings:

Food Item	Amount	Calories	Fat Grams
Creamy Italian (Weight Watchers)	1 Tbsp.	50	5
Italian, mix (Weight Watchers)	1 Tbsp.	0	0
Italian, oil free:			
(Good Seasons)	1 Tbsp.	5	0
(Kraft)	1 Tbsp.	5	0
(Pritikin)	1 Tbsp.	5	0
Vinaigrette (Pritikin)	1 Tbsp.	10	0
Lite Dijon (Wish-Bone)	1 Tbsp.	25	2
Lite Italian (Wish-Bone)	1 Tbsp.	5	trace

Food Item	Amount	Calories	Fat Grams
Reduced-Calorie Zesty (Kraft)	1 Tbsp.	5	trace
Red Wine Vinegar (Featherweight)	1 Tbsp.	5	0
Tomato-Based Low-Calorie Dressings:			
2-Calorie (Featherweight)	1 Tbsp.	2	0
French, oil free			
(El Molino)	1 Tbsp.	10	0
(Pritikin)	1 Tbsp.	10	0
Lite Russian (Wish-Bone)	1 Tbsp.	25	trace
Reduced-Calorie Bacon & Tomato (Kraft)	1 Tbsp.	30	2
Reduced-Calorie Catalina (Kraft)	1 Tbsp.	60	trace
Russian, oil-free (Pritikin)	1 Tbsp.	10	0
Other Dressings:			
Caesar (Wish-Bone)	1 Tbsp.	70	8
French (Kraft)	1 Tbsp.	60	6
French Old Fashioned, mix (Good Seasons)	1 Tbsp.	85	9
Russian (Kraft)	1 Tbsp.	60	5
Sweet and Spicy (Wish-Bone)	1 Tbsp.	70	6
Thousand Island (Wish-Bone)	1 Tbsp.	60	6

SEEDS & NUTS:

Food Item	Amount	Calories	Fat Grams
Almonds:			
Dry-roasted	1 oz.	165	15
Raw	1 oz.	170	15
Cashews, oil-roasted	1 oz.	160	13
Coconut, shredded	1 oz.	55	4
Mixed nuts, oil-roasted	1 oz.	180	17
Peanuts, oil-roasted	1 oz.	165	14
Pecans, dry-roasted	1 oz.	185	19
Pistachios, dry-roasted	1 oz.	160	14

Food Item	Amount	Calories	Fat Grams
Pumpkin Seeds, whole, roasted	1 oz.	150	13
Sesame Seeds, dried	1 oz.	165	14
Sunflower Seeds, shelled	1 oz.	160	14
Walnuts, chopped, raw	1 oz.	170	16

SOUP:

Food Item	Amount	Calories	Fat Grams
Beef Barley	1 cup	320	14
Chicken Noodle	1 cup	75	2
Clam Chowder:			
New England, made with milk	1 cup	165	7
Manhattan	1 cup	80	2
Cream of Broccoli	1 cup	170	9
Cream of Celery	1 cup	90	6
Cream of Chicken	1 cup	115	7
Gazpacho	1 cup	60	2
Lentil	1 cup	140	4
Low-Salt Soups: (Campbell's)			
Chicken and Noodles	7¼ oz.	120	4
Chicken Broth	7¼ oz.	25	2
Chunky Vegetable Beef	7¼ oz.	120	3
Cream of Mushroom	7¼ oz.	130	9
French Onion	1 cup	80	5
Split Pea	7¼ oz.	160	3
Tomato and Tomato Pieces	7¼ oz.	130	4
Minestrone	1 cup	85	1
Split Pea with water	1 cup	190	4
Tomato with water	1 cup	85	2
Vegetable Beef	1 cup	75	2
Wonton	1 cup	105	4

BREAKFAST FOODS:

Food Item	Amount	Calories	Fat Grams
Pancakes:			
(Aunt Jemima)	3 med.	210	2
(Mrs. Smith)	3 med.	230	4

Food Item	Amount	Calories	Fat Grams
Waffles:			
Frozen	1	95	3
Homemade	1 lg.	245	13
Popover, homemade	1	110	3
French toast:			
Frozen	2 slices	195	6
Homemade	2 slices	155	7
Pop-Tart (most varieties)	1 ea.	210	7

SNACK FOODS:

Food Item	Amount	Calories	Fat Grams
Corn Chips	1 oz.	155	10
Popcorn:			
Plain	3 cups	125	1
With oil	3 cups	125	6
Potato Chips	10 ea.	115	7
Pretzels:	1 oz.	110	1
Soft	1 ea.	190	2
Very thin	1 oz.	110	1
Tortilla Chips, round	1 oz.	145	8
Pork Rinds (Frito-Lay)	1 oz.	150	9
Cheese Puffed Balls	1 oz.	160	11

FAST FOODS:

Food Item	Amount	Calories	Fat Grams
Fried Chicken Breast	2.4 oz.	200	12
Fried Chicken Sandwich	1 ea.	600	32
Fried Fish Sandwich	1 ea.	500	27
Hamburger	1 ea.	310	12
Quarter Pounder w/ Cheese	1 ea.	525	32

BIBLIOGRAPHY

American College of Sports Medicine. Position statement on proper and improper weight-loss programs, *Med Sci Sports Exerc,* 15 (1982): ix.

American Diabetic Association. *Exchange Lists for Meal Planning.* Chicago: American Dietetic Association, 1986.

Aravanis, C., A. Corcondilas, A. S. Dontas, et al. "The Greek Islands of Crete and Corfu," *Circulation* 41, suppl. 1 (1970): 1–88.

Blackburn, G., and E. S. Horton. "Introduction: An Overview of the Assessment and Regulation of Energy Balance in Humans," *Am J Clin Nutr* 38 (1983): 972.

Bogardus, C. "Familial Dependance of the Resting Metabolic Rate," *N Eng J Med* 315, No. 2 (July 10, 1986): 96.

Brownell, K. D., M. R. C. Greenwood, E. Stellor, et al. "The Effects of Repeated Cycles of Weight Loss and Regain in Rats," *Physiol Behav* 1986.

Brownell, K. D., and A. J. Stunkard. "Exercise in the Development and Control of Obesity." In A. J. Stunkard, ed., *Obesity.* Philadelphia: W. B. Saunders, 1980.

Burkitt, D. P., and H. C. Trowell. *Refined Carbohydrate Foods and Disease: The Implications of Dietary Fiber.* London: Academic Press, 1975.

Castelli, W. P. "Epidemiology of Coronary Heart Disease: The Framingham Study," *Am J Med* 76, no. 2A (1984): 4.

Committee on Diet and Health, Food and Nutrition Board, and Commission on Life Sciences, National Research Council. *Diet and Health: Implication for Reducing Chronic Disease Risk.* Washington, DC: National Academy Press, 1989.

"Diet Intervention Methods to Reduce Fat Intake: Nutrient

and Food Group Composition of Self-Selected Low-Fat Diets," *J Am Diet Assoc* 90, no. 1 (1990).

Donato, K., and D. M. Hegsted. "Efficiency of Various Sources of Energy for Growth," *Proc Natl Acad Sci* 82 (1985): 486.

Dreon, D. M., B. Frey-Hewitt, N. Ellsworth, et al. "Dietary Fat: Carbohydrate Ratio and Obesity in Middle-Aged Men," *Am J Clin Nutr* 47 (1988): 995.

Dwyer, J. T. *Nutrition Concerns and Problems of the Aged.* New York: Oxford University Press, 1990.

Foster, C. J., R. L. Weinwein, R. Birch, et al. "Obesity and Serum Lipids: An Evaluation of the Relative Contribution of Body Fat and Fat Distribution and Lipid Levels," *Int J Obesity* 11 (1987): 151.

Hagan, R. D., S. J. Upton, L. Wont, et al. "The Effects of Aerobic Conditioning and/or Caloric Restriction in Overweight Men and Women," *Med Sci Sports Exerc* 18 (1986): 87.

Haskell, W. L. "Exercise-Induced Changes in Plasma Lipids and Lipoproteins," *Prev Med* 13 (1984): 23.

Jenkins, D. J. A., T. M. S. Wolever, V. Vuksan, et al. "Nibbling Versus Gorging: Metabolic Advantages of Increased Meal Frequency," *N Engl J Med* 321 (1989): 929.

Kern, P. A., M.D. "The Effects of Weight Loss on the Activity Expression of Adipose Tissue Lipoprotein Lipase in Very Obese Human Beings," *N Engl J Med* 322, no. 15 (April 12, 1990): 1053.

Lissner, L., D. A. Levitsky, B. J. Strupp, et al. "Dietary Fat and the Regulation of Energy in Human Subjects," *Am J Clin Nutr* 46 (1987): 886.

Lohman, T. G. "Skinfolds and Body Density and their Relation to Body Fatness: A Review," *Hum Biol* 53 (1981): 181.

Lukaski, H. C. "Methods for Assessment of Human Body Composition: Traditional and New," *Am J Clin Nutr* 46 (1987): 537.

Mattson, F. H. "A Changing Role for Dietary Monounsaturated Fatty Acids," *J Am Diet Assoc* 89 (1989): 387.

Miller, W. C. "Is Exercise Necessary for Weight Loss?" *Obesity and Health* 4, no. 5 (May 1990).

The Nutrition Committee, American Heart Association. "Dietary Guidelines for Healthy American Adults," *Circulation* 77 (1988): 721A.

Ornish, D. *Stress, Diet, and Your Heart.* New York: Holt, Rinehart & Winston, 1982.

Paffenbarger, R. S., R. T. Hyde, A. L. Wing, et al. "A Natural History of Athleticism and Cardiovascular Health," *JAMA* 252, no. 4 (1984): 491.

Pennington, J. A. *Food Values of Portions Commonly Used* (15th ed.). New York: Harper & Row, 1989.

Pritikin, N. *The Pritikin Program for Diet and Exercise.* New York: Grosset & Dunlap, 1982.

Ravussin, E. "Determinants of 24-Hour Recall Energy Expenditure in Man," *J Clin Investig Inc.* 78 (Dec. 1986): 1568–1578.

"The Substitution of Sucrose Polyester for Dietary Fat in Obese Hypercholesterolemic Outpatients," *Am J Clin Nutr* 1985.

Stunkard, A. J., and T. A. Wadden. "Restrained Eating and Human Obesity," *Nutr Reviews,* 48, no. 2 (Feb. 1990).

Thompson, J. K., G. J. Jarvie, B. B. Lahey, et al. "Exercise and Obesity: Etiology, Physiology and Intervention," *Psychol Bull* 91 (1982): 55.

VanItallie, T. B. "The Perils of Obesity in Middle Aged Women," *N Engl J Med* 322, no. 13 (March 29, 1990): 928–929.

VanItallie, T. B., and H. R. Kissileff. "Physiology of Energy Intake," *Am J Clin Nutr* 42 (1985): 914.

Weisner, R. L., T. A. Wadden, C. Ritenbaugh, et al. "Recommended Therapeutic Guidelines for Professional Weight Control Programs," *Am J Clin Nutr* 40 (1984): 865.

Wood, P. D. "Changes on Plasma Lipids and Lipoproteins in Overweight Men During Weight Loss Through Dieting Compared to Exercise," *N Engl J Med* 319, no. 18 (1988): 1173.

Zuti, W. B. *The Y's Way to Physical Fitness.* Rosemont, IL: YMCA of the USA, 1982.